Catalogue
Spring 2019

The 300th Anniversary of the building.

The Old Corner Book Store, Boston.
Painting, c. 1845 by Margaret Fuller, Wm. D. Ticknor & Co. Books

Brick Tower Press

Habent Sua Fata Libelli

Brick Tower Press
Manhanset House
Dering Harbor, New York 11965-0342
Tel: 212-427-7139
bricktower@aol.com • www.BrickTowerPress.com

Distributed to the trade by Ingram Content Group LLC
One Ingram Blvd.
La Vergne, TN 37086
(615) 793-5000

Retail Stores (U.S.)
Email Customer Service
customerservice@IngramContent.com
(800) 937-8000

Retail Stores (Outside U.S.)
Email Customer Service
customerservice@IngramContent.com
(615) 793-5000, ext. 27652
Christian / Spring Arbor
Email Customer Service
(800) 395-4340

Ingram Publisher Services
Email Customer Service
customerservice@IngramContent.com
1 (866) 400-5351

For sales in the UK and Europe please contact
our distributor,
Gazelle Book Services
Falcon House, Queens Square
Lancaster, LA1 1RN, UK
Tel: (01524) 68765 Fax: (01524) 63232
stef@gazellebooks.co.uk

Please do order our titles directly from us at bricktower@aol.com or from our distributor, Ingram Content.

For general information, please contact
John T. Colby Jr., publisher, at
bricktower@aol.com
Tel: 212-427-7139

For international rights and book club sales, please contact
Bob Diforio
D4EO Literary Agency
bob@d4eo.com
941-226-0500 office
203-545-7180 mobile

For non-literary rights contact either John Colby at
bricktower@aol.com or
Alan Morell at amorell@creativemanagementpartners.com

Featured Title, Page 4

CONTENTS

Brick Tower Press
Habent Sua Fata Libelli

Brick Tower Press
POB 342, Manhanset House
Shelter Island Hts., NY 11965-0342
bricktower@aol.com
www.BrickTowerPress.com

About the Book

"... (Payne) has the gift, as does John Keegan, of using prose to elevate facts, figures, dates and events into the realms of the dramatic."
–Book Reviewer

Based on entirely fresh primary research. Leonardo presents important new information and perspectives on one of the most interesting men and greatest geniuses of all time.

The following are only a few of the new and controversial findings offered by Payne in this highly readable book. The portrait of a bearded man universally accepted as a self-portrait is actually a drawing of Leonardo's father. The subject of the Mona Lisa was not the wife of a merchant but the Duchess of Milan. (Among the illustrations in the book are two earlier, seldom-seen Mona Lisas.) Leonardo was not the son of a peasant woman, as it is generally thought he was, but of a high-born woman.

Payne paints an extraordinarily convincing Picture of Leonardo not only as a giant of his age, but also as a man, human, real, simple and natural. Besides dispelling many myths about him, the author places his subject realistically in his own time–the summit of the Italian Renaissance with its wars and sudden upheavals, its unsurpassed artists and architects, its ambitious and often warring princes. Leonardo is a meticulously accurate book and it reads like a swiftly paced novel.

Leonardo, His Life and Works
by Robert Payne

Library: Robert Payne Library
Art : History/Renaissance

Print price $23.95
438 Pages
ISBN: 9781883283964
Binding: B&W 6 x 9 in or 229 x 152 mm Perfect Bound on Creme w/Gloss Lam
Series Number: 3

Robert Payne (1911-l983) was born in Cornwall, U.K. His father was English, his mother French. He was educated at St. Paul's School in London and at the universities of Liverpool, Capetown in South Africa, Munich and The Sorbonne.

During his lifetime he had over a hundred books published on a wide range of subjects, the widest range of any known author. He was known chiefly for his biographies and history books, among them Hitler, Lenin, Stalin, Gandhi, Leonardo, Chaplin, the Christian Centuries, The World of Art. He also wrote novels and poetry.

Librarians loved him; critics raved about him. Orville Prescott of The New York Times referred to him as "a literary phenomenon of astounding versatility and industry."

Brick Tower Press

Habent Sua Fata Libelli

Brick Tower Press
POB 342, Manhanset House
Shelter Island Hts., NY 11965-0342
bricktower@aol.com
www.BrickTowerPress.com

About the Book

•"Much has been written about firefighters, some of it by people who actually fight fires. Few of the books I have any knowledge of show the mindset of the firefighters with as much insight and candor as this book..." –from the foreword by Hugh Downs

•"Every so often a writer of substantive talent appears through the smokey background to perk up our interest in firefighters and firefighting. George Pickett is just such a man.... In The Brave you will come to know him and a valiant group of men as they speed from alarm to alarm in downtown New York, where the buildings are tall and for the most part old, where bums and drug addicts populate the streets, and where the fire companies hardly ever rest. You will begin to feel that you too are a member of Engine 33, Ladder 9, and, after George's promotion to lieutenant, of some of Brooklyn's busiest fire companies. It is an empowering feeling, until you suddenly realize that these are among the very first fire companies who will arrive one fateful day in their future at the World Trade Center, providing our city with more courage, determination, and selflessness that we ever knew we had. You will then thank George Pickett for letting you into their lives."
–Dennis Smith, New York Times' bestselling author

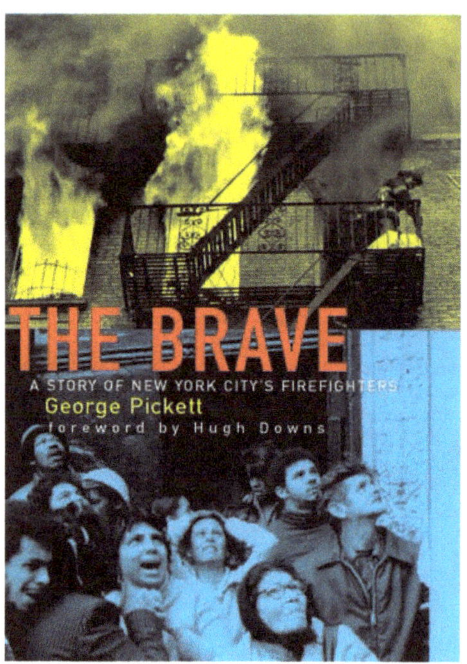

The Brave, a Story of New York City's Firefighters
by George Pickett, Hugh Downs

Biography

Print price $27.95
246 Pages
ISBN: 9781883283377
Binding: B&W 6.14 x 9.21in or 234 x 156mm (Royal 8vo) Blue Cloth w/Jacket on White w/Gloss Lam

Brick Tower Press
Habent Sua Fata Libelli

Brick Tower Press
POB 342, Manhanset House
Shelter Island Hts., NY 11965-0342
bricktower@aol.com
www.BrickTowerPress.com

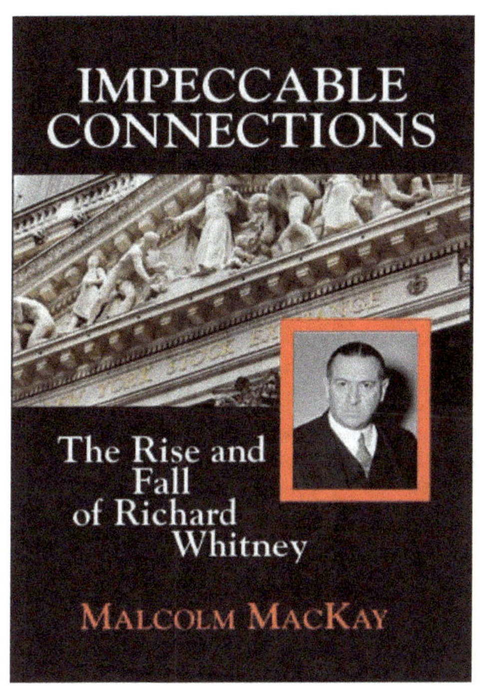

About the Book
"In 'Impeccable Connections,' Malcolm MacKay, who knew his subject, attempts to fathom the man whom puzzled contemporaries could not."
—Maxwell Carter, writing for the The Wall Street Journal

"Read this spellbinding book, which repeatedly takes your breath away, and learn that some things never change."
—Craig R. Whitney, author of LIVING WITH GUNS: A LIBERAL'S CASE FOR THE SECOND AMENDMENT

Although Richard Whitney is not a common name today, the story of his rise to the top of Wall Street and fall to Sing Sing presages the more recent trajectories of men such as Bernard Madoff, Ivan Boesky, and Charles Keating. In a sense, Whitney's fall was even greater in that he started at the top of the old-guard establishment.

"NOT DICK WHITNEY. NOT DICK WHITNEY!" President Franklin D. Roosevelt exclaimed upon being told Richard Whitney, the long-time president of the New York Stock Exchange, was a criminal. Almost ten years earlier, on October 24, 1929, Black Thursday, as one newspaper's headline put it the next day, "Richard Whitney Halts Stock Panic." In 1934, he appeared on the cover of Time magazine, hailed as the leader of the securities industry in its fight against New Deal regulation. Whitney's message was clear: the securities industry could regulate itself, and the federal government should stay out. Sound familiar?

This book tells the tale of Richard Whitney and describes in detail the banking and investment structure that precipitated the stock market collapse of 1929, and how as president of the New York Stock Exchange, Richard Whitney played his role

IMPECCABLE CONNECTIONS is both a biography of an important figure and an excellent primer on the reasons for securities regulations that are in today's headlines.

Malcolm MacKay is a lawyer and businessman who, as a boy and young man, knew Richard Whitney in his post-prison years. MacKay has thought about Whitney, and why he did what he did, all his life. A graduate of Princeton and Harvard Law School, he lives in Brooklyn, New York.

Impeccable Connections: The Rise and Fall of Richard Whitney
by Malcolm MacKay

BIOGRAPHY & AUTOBIOGRAPHY : Business

Print price $12.95
120 Pages
ISBN: 9781883283629
Binding: B&W 6 x 9 in or 229 x 152 mm Perfect Bound on Creme w/Gloss Lam

Brick Tower Press
Habent Sua Fata Libelli

Brick Tower Press
POB 342, Manhanset House
Shelter Island Hts., NY 11965-0342
bricktower@aol.com
www.BrickTowerPress.com

About the Book

Ever since the earliest days of commerce, business people have organized themselves into partnerships. They formed groups with a common interest and worked together as a single unit, assuming both the risks and rewards of the business. It was a natural way of achieving a common goal. If the business succeeded, all of the partners made money. If it flourished, the partners even sometimes became rich. However, success wasn't assured and if the business failed, they all suffered together. In addition to a multitude of other industries, this was the model that dominated how Wall Street firms operated up until the 1980's.

Beginning in the 1980's, it was not uncommon to find that a freshly-hired trainee - a kid literally right out of college - knew more about the new financial instruments than the CEO of the firm that hired him. In some instances, the kids were learning about the finer points of newly-invented instruments before their managers knew they even existed. These were the new breed of traders scattered across the trading desks.

The individuals whose stories compose the contents of this book are some of the smartest people you'll ever read about. They had an intimate understanding of the markets and how best to make money from them, but they also had an equally in-depth knowledge of some of the flaws in the markets. Or sometimes, flaws in the systems at the banks themselves. They used their knowledge to make money. And when that failed, they often used their knowledge of how they system was structured to hide their losses. And when that failed, there was no turning back.

Rogue Traders (HC)
by Scott E.D. Skyrm

BIOGRAPHY & AUTOBIOGRAPHY : Business
Business & Economics : Finance

Print price $35.95
248 Pages
ISBN: 9781590190012

Binding: B&W 6 x 9 in or 229 x 152 mm Blue Cloth w/Jacket on White w/Gloss Lam

Scott E.D. Skyrm is one of the leading figures in the repo and securities finance markets today, and regularly quoted in The Wall Street Journal, The Financial Times, Bloomberg News Service, Reuters, Market News, and Dow Jones.

He is highly regarded as a former salesman, trader, trading desk manager, and global business head in fixed-income, securities finance, and securities clearing and settlement. He recently left Newedge, where he was their "Global Head of Repo, Money Markets, and Fixed Income Clearing."

He now is writing commentaries on the repo market, the short-end of the Treasury market, Federal Reserve policy and general Wall Street topics. He has worked on Wall Street for over 22 years and has taken billion-dollar risks on the trading floor, managed a multi-billion dollar balance sheet, and consistently ran one of the most profitable trading groups at every firm where he worked.

Brick Tower Press

Habent Sua Fata Libelli

Brick Tower Press
POB 342, Manhanset House
Shelter Island Hts., NY 11965-0342
bricktower@aol.com
www.BrickTowerPress.com

About the Book

"... (Payne) has the gift, as does John Keegan, of using prose to elevate facts, figures, dates and events into the realms of the dramatic."
—Book Reviewer

"While comparatively little is known about William Shakespeare himself, one of the world's authentic geniuses, there is a great deal known about the age in which he lived. Robert Payne has blended the little and the lot into a most appealing and memorable work. The parts dealing with the theatre of Shakespeare's time are especially vivid, as are some of the anecdotes which have survived the passage of centuries. Payne is to be congratulated." —Robert Cromie, author/critic

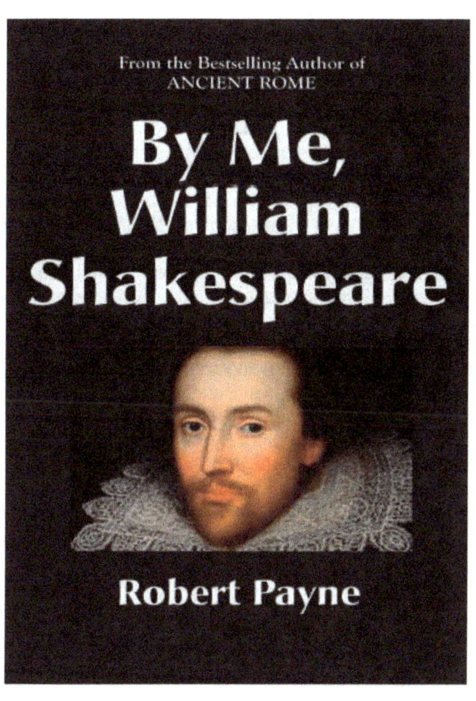

By Me, William Shakespeare
by Robert Payne

Library: Robert Payne Library
Biography & Autobiography : Composers & Musicians

Print price $29.95
510 Pages
ISBN: 9781883283988
Binding: B&W 6 x 9 in or 229 x 152 mm Perfect Bound on Creme w/Gloss Lam
Series Number: 2

Robert Payne (1911-l983) was born in Cornwall, U.K. His father was English, his mother French. He was educated at St. Paul's School in London and at the universities of Liverpool, Capetown in South Africa, Munich and The Sorbonne.

During his lifetime he had over a hundred books published on a wide range of subjects, the widest range of any known author. He was known chiefly for his biographies and history books, among them Hitler, Lenin, Stalin, Gandhi, Leonardo, Chaplin, the Christian Centuries, The World of Art. He also wrote novels and poetry.

Librarians loved him; critics raved about him. Orville Prescott of The New York Times referred to him as "a literary phenomenon of astounding versatility and industry."

Brick Tower Press

Habent Sua Fata Libelli

Brick Tower Press
POB 342, Manhanset House
Shelter Island Hts., NY 11965-0342
bricktower@aol.com
www.BrickTowerPress.com

About the Book

"... (Payne) has the gift, as does John Keegan, of using prose to elevate facts, figures, dates and events into the realms of the dramatic."
–Book Reviewer

NO ONE LIVING IN NEW YORK CAN escape from George Gershwin. His music still comes in unrestrained and sometimes paralyzing abundance through the radio. Its gaiety, its flippancy, its violence, its electrifying "blues" passages, though written in the twenties and early thirties, still reflect the prevailing mood of New York. No other city could have produced him, and no other city has taken him so much to its heart.

Robert Payne's first motive for writing his story was because he planned to write a long novel about New York, and wanted to get to grips with that strange, effervescent period when New York was still young and reckless. Gershwin was, he thought, the best symbol of the twenties. In the novel someone very like him was to grow old and grey with the weariness of his eternal youth, dying at last in a quarrel in a Bowery doss-house. It was a satisfying ending, but Gershwin's ending was still more satisfying.

George Gershwin was larger than life, and no one was ever so demanding. They said of him that he was like a young Prince, and nothing he ever asked for was refused him. Perhaps that was the tragedy, for certainly the stereotype of the brilliantly successful composer was not entirely satisfactory. So Robert Payne has painted him in the limelight, but also as he walked through the Shadows.

Gershwin
by Robert Payne

Library: Robert Payne Library
Biography & Autobiography : Composers & Musicians

Print price $14.95
138 Pages
ISBN: 9781883283933
Binding: B&W 6 x 9 in or 229 x 152 mm Perfect Bound on Creme w/Gloss Lam
Series Number: 5

Robert Payne (1911-l983) was born in Cornwall, U.K. His father was English, his mother French. He was educated at St. Paul's School in London and at the universities of Liverpool, Capetown in South Africa, Munich and The Sorbonne.

During his lifetime he had over a hundred books published on a wide range of subjects, the widest range of any known author. He was known chiefly for his biographies and history books, among them Hitler, Lenin, Stalin, Gandhi, Leonardo, Chaplin, the Christian Centuries, The World of Art. He also wrote novels and poetry.

Librarians loved him; critics raved about him. Orville Prescott of The New York Times referred to him as "a literary phenomenon of astounding versatility and industry."

Brick Tower Press

Habent Sua Fata Libelli

Brick Tower Press
POB 342, Manhanset House
Shelter Island Hts., NY 11965-0342
bricktower@aol.com
www.BrickTowerPress.com

About the Book

This is a fascinating inside story about one prolific songwriter's experience working for the famed Motown Records and directly with Motown's founder Berry Gordy. It is an interesting look into the actual contracts between Mr. Gordy and his talented "family" of musicians told by one of the most famous songwriters of his time. If Motown didn't grow to be the success it is today, Motown's royalty contract—work-for-hire—compensation would be fair under the circumstances. The difficulty comes when Mr. Gordy's success as a businessman exceeds every possible prediction.

The FAME WITHOUT FORTUNE story begins in 1959 with Al Cleveland as a young man who makes the hard choice to leave his wife and children behind in order to chase his dreams of being a singer and a songwriter. It follows him through the trials of New York City and putting up with discrimination on the "Chitlin' Circuit." There he has an adulterous affair sending the final blow to his marriage. A short time later, he marries his second wife and Al's big break seemed to come when he signed up with Motown Records under Berry Gordy. He was writing number-one songs for stars such as Smokey Robinson and Marvin Gaye. All along his fame grew, but he was not receiving pay for them. Instead he received headaches, heartaches, excuses, and IRS raids. He left Motown and toured with famous artists, but during that time, there was little room for a black songwriter to make a living. Al had to return to Motown to stay in the business.

Fame Without Fortune, Motown Records, the Al Cleveland Story
by Daryl Cleveland, Glenn Soucy

Biography & Autobiography : Composers & Musicians

Print price $21.95
306 Pages
ISBN: 9781883283841
Binding: B&W 6 x 9 in or 229 x 152 mm Perfect Bound on White w/Gloss Lam

Brick Tower Press
Habent Sua Fata Libelli

Brick Tower Press
POB 342, Manhanset House
Shelter Island Hts., NY 11965-0342
bricktower@aol.com
www.BrickTowerPress.com

About the Book

THE WAY OF THE PIRATE is a fascinating look at the men that raided the seas and the women, kings, and countries that aided, supported, hunted, and condemned them. Captain Edward Teach, more famously known as Blackbeard, Captain Kidd, and Sir Francis Drake are among the 1,150 pirates, buccaneers, and privateers whose adventure is told.

THE WAY OF THE PIRATE also reveals the colorful pirate way of life including the fascinating "Articles of Agreement" that governed a pirate's life aboard ship. From captain to lowly mate, from cutlass and cannon to pistols and muskets, THE WAY OF THE PIRATE is a benchmark one-volume account of the most romantic adventurers in maritime history.

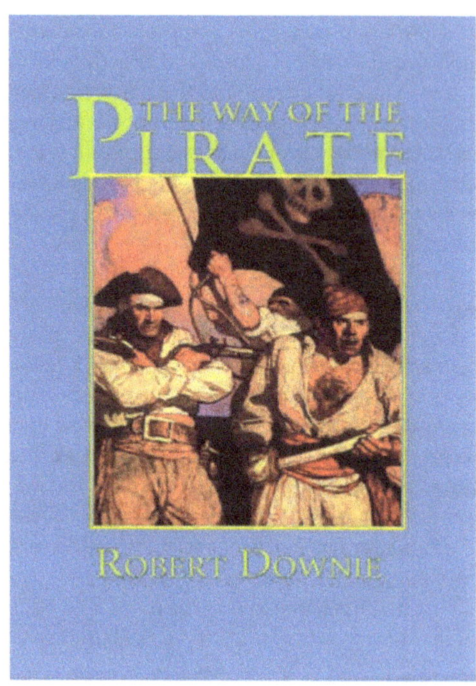

The Way of the Pirate
by Robert Downie

Biography & Autobiography : Criminals & Outlaws
Biography

Print price $13.95
270 Pages
ISBN: 9781883283490
Binding: B&W 6 x 9 in or 229 x 152 mm Perfect Bound on Creme w/Gloss Lam

Brick Tower Press
POB 342, Manhanset House
Shelter Island Hts., NY 11965-0342
bricktower@aol.com
www.BrickTowerPress.com

About the Book

"... (Payne) has the gift, as does John Keegan, of using prose to elevate facts, figures, dates and events into the realms of the dramatic."
–Book Reviewer

Robert Payne has succeeded in a difficult task: he can convey in words the magic of great clowning. His book was justly described, in the Saturday Review of Literature, as ranking "with the best writings on Chaplin in any language." We learn, Incidentally, a lot about Chaplin himself–about his precarious London childhood, his early stage work, his experiences with Fred Karno and Mack Sennett in the earliest screen comedies–but it is 'Charlie' who holds the centre of the stage.

Robert Payne analzses all his important appearances on the screen, and also traces his descent back through Dan Leno, Grimaldi, Pierrot and Punch, to the earliest laughter-maker of them all.

The Great Charlie, the Biography of the Tramp
by Robert Payne

Library: Robert Payne Library
Biography & Autobiography : Entertainment & Performing Arts

Print price $19.95
304 Pages
ISBN: 9781883283957
Binding: B&W 6 x 9 in or 229 x 152 mm Perfect Bound on Creme w/Gloss Lam
Series Number: 4

Robert Payne (1911-l983) was born in Cornwall, U.K. His father was English, his mother French. He was educated at St. Paul's School in London and at the universities of Liverpool, Capetown in South Africa, Munich and The Sorbonne.

During his lifetime he had over a hundred books published on a wide range of subjects, the widest range of any known author. He was known chiefly for his biographies and history books, among them Hitler, Lenin, Stalin, Gandhi, Leonardo, Chaplin, the Christian Centuries, The World of Art. He also wrote novels and poetry.

Librarians loved him; critics raved about him. Orville Prescott of The New York Times referred to him as "a literary phenomenon of astounding versatility and industry."

Brick Tower Press

Habent Sua Fata Libelli

Brick Tower Press
POB 342, Manhanset House
Shelter Island Hts., NY 11965-0342
bricktower@aol.com
www.BrickTowerPress.com

About the Book

"More than KILLING PATTON"–A Reviewer

This is the story of the life and mind of George C. Marshall, soldier and statesman, as told by a distinguished writer whose own background makes him particularly qualified to discuss some of the more controversial aspects of General Marshall's work since World War II.
Showing in quite an extraordinary way how Marshall represents the strengths and weaknesses of the American tradition, this book's study of the life of a great contemporary American illuminates the American scene with an insight rarely equaled in a biographical work.

The Marshall Story is neither a "white wash" of General Marshall nor an attack on him. His errors of judgment are studied at some length, partly because the same pattern of behavior is visible in each of these errors, but chiefly because the consequences of error were disastrous. But against these errors are set his triumphs: the first a personal one, the others impersonal and prodigiously important because they affected the conduct of the war and the conduct of the peace–his generalship and the Marshall Plan.

In this book, Robert Payne's subject is a man who has been described by President Harry S Truman as "the greatest living American." And Payne's treatment of the subject makes The Marshall Story a study of a man who knew exactly where he was going, went there, made mistakes, and seemed perhaps not to belong to our own time. This book will shatter some illusions about George C. Marshall, but it will also place him in the perspective of his time and demonstrate that he may be even greater than many of us have thought him to be.

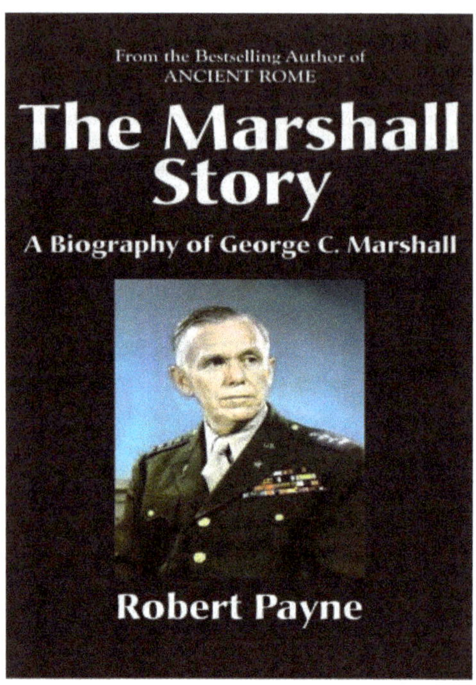

The Marshall Story, A Biography of General George C. Marshall
by Robert Payne

Library: Robert Payne Library
Biography & Autobiography : Military

Print price $26.95
370 Pages
ISBN: 9781883283940
Binding: B&W 6 x 9 in or 229 x 152 mm Perfect Bound on White w/Gloss Lam
Series Number: 6

Robert Payne (1911-l983) was born in Cornwall, U.K. His father was English, his mother French. He was educated at St. Paul's School in London and at the universities of Liverpool, Capetown in South Africa, Munich and The Sorbonne.

During his lifetime he had over a hundred books published on a wide range of subjects, the widest range of any known author. He was known chiefly for his biographies and history books, among them Hitler, Lenin, Stalin, Gandhi, Leonardo, Chaplin, the Christian Centuries, The World of Art. He also wrote novels and poetry.

Librarians loved him; critics raved about him. Orville Prescott of The New York Times referred to him as "a literary phenomenon of astounding versatility and industry."

Brick Tower Press

Habent Sua Fata Libelli

Brick Tower Press
POB 342, Manhanset House
Shelter Island Hts., NY 11965-0342
bricktower@aol.com
www.BrickTowerPress.com

About the Book
"More than KILLING PATTON"—A Reviewer

This is the story of the life and mind of George C. Marshall, soldier and statesman, as told by a distinguished writer whose own background makes him particularly qualified to discuss some of the more controversial aspects of General Marshall's work since World War II.

Showing in quite an extraordinary way how Marshall represents the strengths and weaknesses of the American tradition, this book's study of the life of a great contemporary American illuminates the American scene with an insight rarely equalled in a biographical work. The Marshall Story is neither a "white wash" of General Marshall nor an attack on him. His errors of judgment are studied at some length, partly because the same pattern of behavior is visible in each of these errors, but chiefly because the consequences of error were disastrous. But against these errors are set his triumphs: the first a personal one, the others impersonal and prodigiously important because they affected the conduct of the war and the conduct of the peace—his generalship and the Marshall Plan.

In this book, Robert Payne's subject is a man who has been described by President Harry S Truman as "the greatest living American." And Payne's treatment of the subject makes The Marshall Story a study of a man who knew exactly where he was going, went there, made mistakes, and seemed perhaps not to belong to our own time. This book will shatter some illusions about George C. Marshall, but it will also place him in the perspective of his time and demonstrate that he may be even greater than many of us have thought him to be.

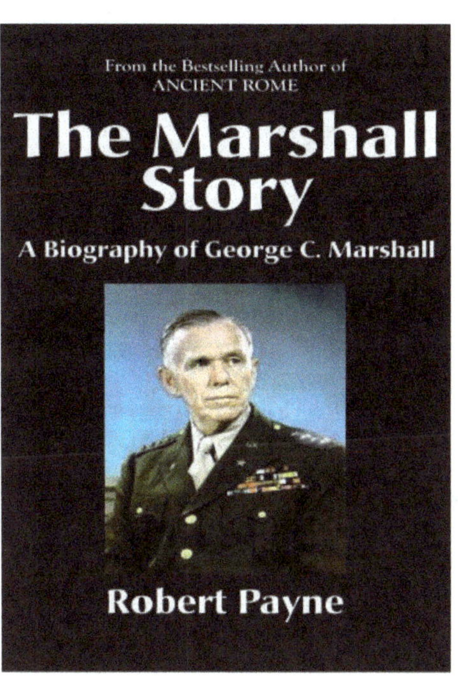

The Marshall Story, A Biography of General George C. Marshall (HC)
by Robert Payne

Library: Robert Payne Library
Biography & Autobiography : Military

Print price $49.95
370 Pages
ISBN: 9781899694525

Binding: B&W 6 x 9 in or 229 x 152 mm Blue Cloth w/Jacket on White w/Gloss Lam
Series Number: 6

Robert Payne (1911-l983) was born in Cornwall, U.K. His father was English, his mother French. He was educated at St. Paul's School in London and at the universities of Liverpool, Capetown in South Africa, Munich and The Sorbonne.

During his lifetime he had over a hundred books published on a wide range of subjects, the widest range of any known author. He was known chiefly for his biographies and history books, among them Hitler, Lenin, Stalin, Gandhi, Leonardo, Chaplin, the Christian Centuries, The World of Art. He also wrote novels and poetry.

Librarians loved him; critics raved about him. Orville Prescott of The New York Times referred to him as "a literary phenomenon of astounding versatility and industry."

Brick Tower Press
Habent Sua Fata Libelli

Brick Tower Press
POB 342, Manhanset House
Shelter Island Hts., NY 11965-0342
bricktower@aol.com
www.BrickTowerPress.com

About the Book
Except for Douglas MacArthur, Theodore Roosevelt Jr. is the most decorated soldier in American history, having earned his Congressional Medal of Honor and every other medal offered by the United States to the foot soldier for combat heroism.

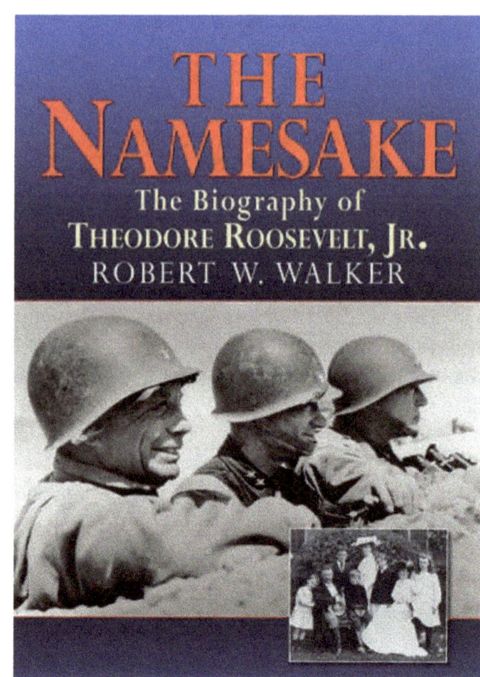

As a young man, he wanted to have a career in the military, but his father, President Theodore Roosevelt, discouraged this. Ted went to Harvard, and dreamed of one day following his father into the White House. Things did not go well for him politically; he had only two one-year terms in the New York State Assembly and a failed run for the New York Governorship. Other positions held in his working life included: carpet salesman, bond salesman, investment banker, Assistant Secretary of the Navy, big game hunter, Governor General of Puerto Rico, Governor General of the Phillipine Islands, and editor and VP at Doubleday Publishing Co. Yet the army was where his niche obviously lay: he served as Battalion Commander in WWI; after the Armistice, he and four other non-career officers founded The American Legion, as it exists today. After seeing combat in North Africa, Sicily and Italy (under Eisenhower) during WWII, he assisted in the preparation for D-Day. On Utah Beach in Normandy, under enemy fire for hours, Roosevelt served as assistant Division Commander of the 4th Infantry Division. His death, some weeks after D-Day, came just before he was to be promoted to Major General, an unheard-of-honor for any reserve officer.

Robert Walker has written the most sympathetic and first full scale biography of Theodore Roosevelt, Jr. since the publication of his wife s autobiography, Day Before Yesterday, fifty years ago. Utilizing the letters of the Roosevelt family as well as TRJr s military records in both World Wars courtesy of the Freedom of Information Act, Walker documents TRJr s courage and fortitude in combat at

The Namesake, the Biography of Theodore Roosevelt Jr.
by Robert W. Walker

Biography & Autobiography : Military
Biography & Autobiography : Rich & Famous
History : Military - World War II
Print price $24.95
354 Pages
ISBN: 9781590190036
Binding: B&W 6 x 9 in or 229 x 152 mm Perfect Bound on White w/Gloss Lam

Brick Tower Press
Habent Sua Fata Libelli

Brick Tower Press
POB 342, Manhanset House
Shelter Island Hts., NY 11965-0342
bricktower@aol.com
www.BrickTowerPress.com

About the Book

Except for Douglas MacArthur, Theodore Roosevelt Jr. is the most decorated soldier in American history, having earned his Congressional Medal of Honor and every other medal offered by the United States to the foot soldier for combat heroism.

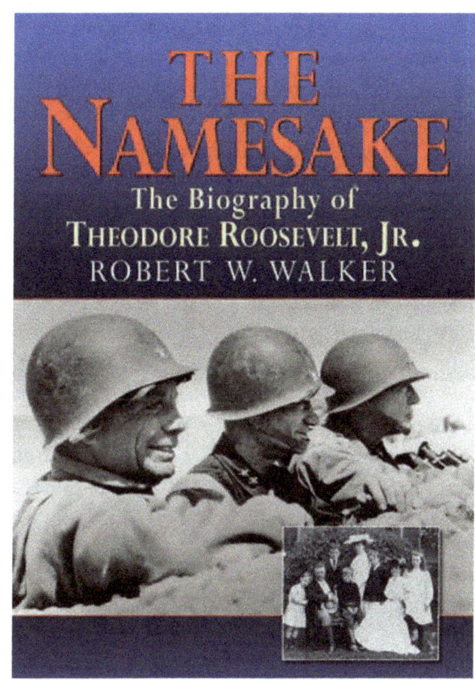

As a young man, he wanted to have a career in the military, but his father, President Theodore Roosevelt, discouraged this. Ted went to Harvard, and dreamed of one day following his father into the White House. Things did not go well for him politically; he had only two one-year terms in the New York State Assembly and a failed run for the New York Governorship. Other positions held in his working life included: carpet salesman, bond salesman, investment banker, Assistant Secretary of the Navy, big game hunter, Governor General of Puerto Rico, Governor General of the Phillipine Islands, and editor and VP at Doubleday Publishing Co. Yet the army was where his niche obviously lay: he served as Battalion Commander in WWI; after the Armistice, he and four other non-career officers founded The American Legion, as it exists today. After seeing combat in North Africa, Sicily and Italy (under Eisenhower) during WWII, he assisted in the preparation for D-Day. On Utah Beach in Normandy, under enemy fire for hours, Roosevelt served as assistant Division Commander of the 4th Infantry Division. His death, some weeks after D-Day, came just before he was to be promoted to Major General, an unheard-of-honor for any reserve officer.

Robert Walker has written the most sympathetic and first full scale biography of Theodore Roosevelt, Jr. since the publication of his wife s autobiography, Day Before Yesterday, fifty years ago. Utilizing the letters of the Roosevelt family as well as TRJr s military records in both World Wars courtesy of the Freedom of Information Act, Walker documents TRJr s courage and fortitude in combat at

The Namesake, The Biography of Theodore Roosevelt Jr. (HC)
by Robert W. Walker

Biography & Autobiography : Military
Biography & Autobiography : Rich & Famous
History : Military - World War II
Print price $37.95
354 Pages
ISBN: 9781596874978
Binding: B&W 6 x 9 in or 229 x 152 mm Case Laminate on White w/Gloss Lam

Brick Tower Press

Habent Sua Fata Libelli

Brick Tower Press
POB 342, Manhanset House
Shelter Island Hts., NY 11965-0342
bricktower@aol.com
www.BrickTowerPress.com

About the Book

- "The best is the best and we must take it on the rare occasions that we find it." –Jim Harrison, Kermit Lynch Wine Merchant News
- "Delicious Reading" -Patrick Kuh, San Francisco Chronicle
- "Funny" –Gourmet Magazine
- "Awe-Inspiring" -Tara Q. Thomas, Wine & Spirits
- "... downright brilliant.." –Mark Bittman, New York Times Book Review
- "Mr. Olney's influence in the culinary profession was profound...." -R.W. Apple Jr., New York Times
- "...an unparalleled view of French food and wine." -William Rice, Chicago Tribune
- "Richard Olney, one of the most influential cookbook writers of his generation...." -Russ Parsons, Los Angeles Times
- "Olney was well ahead of his time. He was without doubt, one of the most influential of modern writers about food. He has a very strong claim to be considered the best." -Times, London
- "Richard Olney's writings may come to share the position bestowed upon A. Escoffier's 1903 Guide Culinaire as the international authoritative culinary text of the 20th century. A pair well-matched, Escoffier preached "Faites simple" and devoted his career to eradicating the excessive culinary follies invented by his predecessors." -Nora Carey, Independent, London
- "Although he was an American, Richard Olney...was one of the foremost writers on French food and wine.... He was admired and respected by the French gastronomic community...." -Jill Norman, Guardian, Manchester
- "He was not as famous as Julia Child...but he was in many ways just as influential...the expatriot theorist who revolutionized the way the best American chefs think about food." -Donald Kaul, Des Moines Register

This book begins in New York in 1951 where Olney, a struggling artist, waited tables in Greenwich Village, then moves to Paris and weaves a magical description of food that becomes so real--as if you were actually there with Olney. It is a long-awaited story of the man who brought the simplicity of French cooking to the United States, and a statement about one of the finest and most important food professionals in the world.

Reflexions-Richard Olney
by Richard Olney

Biography & Autobiography : Personal Memoirs

Print price $27.95
418 Pages
ISBN: 9781883283438
Binding: B&W 6 x 9 in or 229 x 152 mm Perfect Bound on Creme w/Gloss Lam

Brick Tower Press
Habent Sua Fata Libelli

Brick Tower Press
POB 342, Manhanset House
Shelter Island Hts., NY 11965-0342
bricktower@aol.com
www.BrickTowerPress.com

About the Book

In THE LIFE AND DEATH OF ADOLF HITLER, biographer Robert Payne unravels the tangled threads of Hitler's public and private life and looks behind the caricature with the Charlie Chaplin mustache and the unruly shock of hair to reveal a Hitler possessed of immense personal charm that impressed both men and women and brought followers and contributions to the burgeoning Nazi Party. Although he misread his strength and organized an ill-fated putsch, Hitler spent his months in prison writing MEIN KAMPF, which increased his following. Once in undisputed command of the Party, Hitler renounced the chastity of his youth and began a sordid affair with his niece, whose suicide prompted him to reject forever all conventional morality. He promised anything to prospective supporters, then cold-bloodedly murdered them before they could claim a share of the power he reserved for himself. Once he became Chancellor, Hitler step by step bent the powers of the state to his own purposes to satisfy his private fantasies, rearming Germany, slaughtering his real or imaginary enemies, blackmailing one by one the leaders of Europe, and plunging the world into the holocaust of World War II.

THE LIFE AND DEATH OF ADOLF HITLER is the story of not so much a man corrupted by power as a corrupt man who achieved absolute power and used it to an unprecedented degree, knowing at every moment exactly what he was doing and calculating his enemies' weaknesses to a hair's breadth. It is the story of a living man.

The Life and Death of Adolf Hitler (HC)
by Robert Payne

Library: Robert Payne Library
Biography & Autobiography : Presidents and Heads of State

Print price $85
678 Pages
ISBN: 9781883283919
Binding: B&W 6.14 x 9.21 in or 234 x 156mm (Royal 8vo) Blue Cloth w/Jacket on White w/Gloss Lam
Series Number: 8

Robert Payne (1911-l983) was born in Cornwall, U.K. His father was English, his mother French. He was educated at St. Paul's School in London and at the universities of Liverpool, Capetown in South Africa, Munich and The Sorbonne.

During his lifetime he had over a hundred books published on a wide range of subjects, the widest range of any known author. He was known chiefly for his biographies and history books, among them Hitler, Lenin, Stalin, Gandhi, Leonardo, Chaplin, the Christian Centuries, The World of Art. He also wrote novels and poetry.

Librarians loved him; critics raved about him. Orville Prescott of The New York Times referred to him as "a literary phenomenon of astounding versatility and industry."

Brick Tower Press
POB 342, Manhanset House
Shelter Island Hts., NY 11965-0342
bricktower@aol.com
www.BrickTowerPress.com

About the Book

"A practical useful book that will stay on my bookshelf." –Armchairinterviews.com, Bob Pike CSP, CPAE-Speakers Hall of Fame

"For quick and helpful pointers, check out PRESENTATION S.O.S." –TIME Magazine

"This nifty little how-to manual is perfect for people who do stand-up in business." –Joyce Lain Kennedy, Tribune Media Services

An informative and insightful 'must-buy' for readers who sometimes struggle with public speaking...quick, concise and fun." –Today's Black Woman

If you're going to speak in public, or use public speaking to market your business, this is a must-read book." –Isabel M. Isidro, PowerHomeBiz.co

Creating a powerful connection with an audience is one of the most guilt-free, indulgent pleasures that the professional world has to offer.

It can be satisfying and mood elevating, as well as a career-enhancing experience, to create a strong connection with the audience. I'm going to give you instructions that are easy to follow, show examples of how to make them work, and offer lots of encouragement along the way. My goal is to move you from the feelings of dread, if that's where you are, to feelings of excited anticipation for your next presentation. I've based all of these lessons, tips, and examples on my experiences as a broadcast journalist, media production company entrepreneur, and presentation skills coach. No research, studies, or data were harmed or even consulted in the creation of this book. I'm going to tell you exactly what I see working successfully with my clients every day.

Presentation S.O.S.: From Perspiration to Persuasion in 9 Easy Steps
by Mark Wiskup

Business & Economics : Business Communication/Meetings & Presentations

Print price $14.95
122 Pages
ISBN: 9781883283728
Binding: B&W 6 x 9 in or 229 x 152 mm Perfect Bound on White w/Gloss Lam

MARK WISKUP is a professional communications coach and the president of Wiskup Communications. He travels the country extensively, working with executives, managers, sales teams, and customer service personnel. He has been a television news journalist and a media production company owner, and holds degrees from UCLA and Northwestern University. He lives in Tampa, Florida, with his wife, Renee. He is proud not only to be the father of two children, but also of the fact that he once served as a driver for Ian Anderson and the rock band Jethro Tull.

Brick Tower Press
Habent Sua Fata Libelli

Brick Tower Press
POB 342, Manhanset House
Shelter Island Hts., NY 11965-0342
bricktower@aol.com
www.BrickTowerPress.com

About the Book

The summer of 1840, and Boston Harbor is thrumming with politicians, business people, civic leaders, members of the judiciary, and the public. The city is ready for a celebration, and its citizens are waiting impatiently for the arrival of a new age. The elegant Britannia finally enters the harbor loaded with mail from England ushering in the Age of Steam to the Atlantic. This event crystallizes Samuel Cunard's vision and the world will never be the same.

This is the story of a man born and raised in Halifax, Nova Scotia, whose father and mother fled colonial New York after the American Revolution, and became one the most powerful forces of international trade in the nineteenth century. His innovative steamship Britannia was the first reliable, timely link between the Old World and the New, and the transatlantic transportation of mail, goods, and passengers was revolutionized. The continued success of the Cunard Line is a testament to Samuel Cunard's brilliance as both a mariner and a businessman.

The first full-length biography of one of the most fascinating figures in mercantile history, Steam Lion is an important and engaging record of a man, his business, and his times.

Steam Lion : A Biography of Samual Cunard
by John G. Langley

Business & Economics : Corporate & Business History - General
Biography & Autobiography : Business
Business & Economics : Industries - Transportation
Print price $19.95
200 Pages
ISBN: 9781899694754
Binding: B&W 6 x 9 in or 229 x 152 mm Perfect Bound on White w/Gloss Lam

Retired Lawyer John G. Langley, QC, is the worldwide authority on Samuel Cunard. He founded the Cunard Steamship Society, dedicated to the preservation and exchange of historical information and memorabilia pertaining to the Cunard Steamship Company and Cunard himself, in 1998, and he has been consultant to producers of films and documentaries on the life of Cunard. He lives in Halifax, Canada.

Brick Tower Press

Habent Sua Fata Libelli

Brick Tower Press
POB 342, Manhanset House
Shelter Island Hts., NY 11965-0342
bricktower@aol.com
www.BrickTowerPress.com

About the Book

"Daniella has compiled a diverse and distinct set of experiences and views as she helps the reader assess perspectives in risk."

—Connie Lindsey, Executive Vice President,
Head of Corporate Social Responsibility and Global Diversity and Inclusion,
Northern Trust

"Every time a woman chooses security and the safe bet over something new, she is missing the opportunity to achieve greater success and fulfillment in work and in life. Ready, Set...RISK! is filled with real-life stories that are engaging and inspiring....a very practical guide to developing the confidence and the ability to take calculated risks that lead to great reward."

— Debbie Storey, Senior Vice President,
Talent Development and
Chief Diversity Officer, AT&T

In general, women approach career-related decisions that entail risk differently than men do, and take fewer risks in their careers than men do. Are you the type of person who regularly takes career risks but is disappointed with returns, or someone who does not take career risks because you are concerned about the consequences? Do you only have an appetite for limited risk so need every career risk to count, or are you a serial career risk taker who wishes to set new highs in your risk-taking returns as you progress in your career? In this book Daniella Levitt explores why risk taking is an essential part of any woman's career management and advancement strategy. Ready, Set...RISK! is the indispensable 'how to' of successful risk taking in your career.

Ready, Set...Risk!
by Daniella Levitt

Business & Economics : Entrepreneurship

Print price $18.95
224 Pages
ISBN: 9781899694013
Binding: B&W 6 x 9 in or 229 x 152 mm Perfect Bound on White w/Gloss Lam

Daniella Levitt grew up in South Africa. Her passion is empowering transformational change. When she was twenty-six, Daniella moved to the United States. After eleven years with Deloitte Consulting she decided to leave in the year she was up for Partner, and joined Aon Consulting as a Senior Vice President. After Aon, Daniella founded two successful companies. Ovation Global Strategies assists corporations with complex transformational change initiatives, and Daniella Levitt Enterprises focuses on development and advancement of women in the workplace—specifically leveraging strategies around risk taking and cross-generational collaboration.

Brick Tower Press
Habent Sua Fata Libelli

Brick Tower Press
POB 342, Manhanset House
Shelter Island Hts., NY 11965-0342
bricktower@aol.com
www.BrickTowerPress.com

About the Book
RECALCULATING,
97 EXPERTS ON DRIVING SMALL BUSINESS GROWTH offers strategic, tactical, tested solutions to a variety of problems and from a multitude of expert sources.

These senior-level contributors are sector stakeholders, advisors, and practitioners. Their chosen topics address the most common issues, problems, and opportunities identified, continuously requested by readers to the editors of Small Business Digest during the past 15+ years.
Many of the solutions have come from experts who have appeared in SBD's publications, radio programs, and conferences. They were asked to write special 1000-word contributions for the book based on their expertise.

Among the companies represented by senior level contributors are HP, Yellow Pages, Staples, GoDaddy, and Intuit.

Topics covered range from better sales management to moving to the cloud to better financing options. Space is also devoted to management problems, benefits needs, and leadership issues.
Each contributor brings a unique slant to common and not so common questions involving finance, sales, marketing, operation, technology, personnel management, and benefits maximization.

Recalculating, 97+ Experts on Driving Small Business Growth
by JoAnn Laing

Business & Economics : Entrepreneurship

Print price $23.95
336 Pages
ISBN: 9781899694655
Binding: B&W 6 x 9 in or 229 x 152 mm Perfect Bound on White w/Gloss Lam

JoAnn M. Laing has 20+ years of experience envisioning, building and leveraging digital media, technology and information to increase sales, market share and profitability advising small businesses on how to grow. Ms. Laing is skilled in digital and multi-channel marketing. She was named a top woman in Silicon Alley and included in Folio's Top Women in Digital Media.

Donald P. Mazzella is COO and Editorial Director of Information Strategies, Inc. (ISI), a company that helps small business managers, HR professionals, and healthcare industry stakeholders improve profits. He currently oversees an Internet publication network with more than 4.5 million opt-in small business readers and a million more stakeholders in HR and healthcare. His latest book is AN AMERICAN FAMILY SAMPLER from ibooks, Inc.; he co-authored a book on marketing to small business, THE JANUS PRINCIPLE, FOCUSING YOUR

Brick Tower Press
POB 342, Manhanset House
Shelter Island Hts., NY 11965-0342
bricktower@aol.com
www.BrickTowerPress.com

About the Book

"Bigger is better turned out to be another 20th century myth. Larry Farrell has eloquently described why."
–Peter Drucker, The 20th Century's Greatest Management Thinker

"If you want to learn about international entrepreneurism, Larry Farrell is your man."
–Tom Peters, The World's All-time Best Selling Business Author

There's nothing like a severe, unexpected, worldwide recession to get one's entrepreneurial juices flowing. After the initial shock and trauma pass, it finally hits home that you can't trust anyone to run the damn economy and save your job...you're truly on your own in this crazy and uncertain 21st century global economy!

The New Entrepreneurial Age
by Larry Farrell

Business & Economics : Entrepreneurship

Print price $26.95
502 Pages
ISBN: 9781883283889
Binding: B&W 6 x 9 in or 229 x 152 mm Perfect Bound on Creme w/Matte Lam

Larry C. Farrell is the Chairman of The Farrell Company, the world's leading firm for researching and teaching entrepreneurship. He founded the firm in 1983 to do his own ground-breaking research into the high-growth business practices of the world's great entrepreneurs. Today, with affiliates in North America, Asia, Europe, South America, and Africa, over five million people, in forty countries, across nine languages, have attended the company's programs. Over the past quarter century, Larry has personally taught entrepreneurship to more individuals, organizations, and governments than any person in the world.

Brick Tower Press

Habent Sua Fata Libelli

Brick Tower Press
POB 342, Manhanset House
Shelter Island Hts., NY 11965-0342
bricktower@aol.com
www.BrickTowerPress.com

About the Book

"This remarkable book will change the way you look at fixing Wall Street and redeeming capitalism."
– Scott Umstead, President, Fusion Investment Group

Fed up with Wall Street? You're not alone. It doesn't have to be this way! Craig Columbus and Mark Hendrickson turn the subject of financial reform upside down. The authors pull no punches, taking both Wall Street and central bankers to task. They also show you a different side of the financial system, reminding us of the good Wall Street is capable of doing. This hopeful book connects the head and the heart of free markets–uncovering original solutions that cannot be reached by regulations alone. Written for the financial professional and layman alike, GOD AND MAN ON WALL STREET will both challenge and inspire you.

https://plus.google.com/u/0/117681616430711223508/videos#117681616430711223508/videos

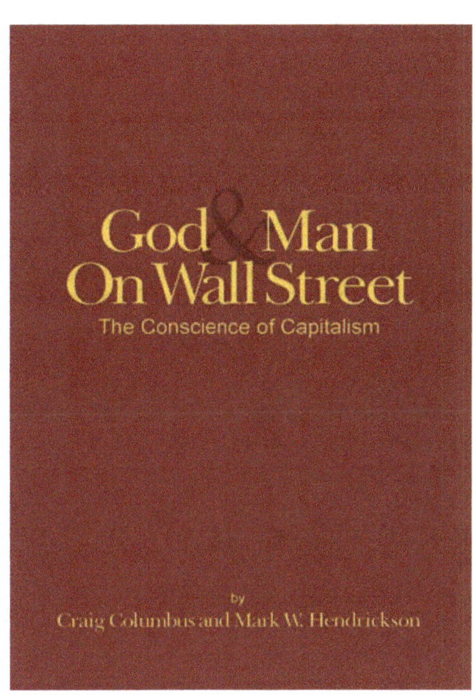

God and Man on Wall Street, The Conscience of Capitalism
by Mark Hendrickson

Business & Economics : Finance

Print price $17.95
196 Pages
ISBN: 9781883283797
Binding: B&W 6 x 9 in or 229 x 152 mm Perfect Bound on White w/Gloss Lam

A frequent commentator on financial television for fifteen years, Craig Columbus is one of Wall Street's most recognizable strategists and financial executives. He also serves as the chair of the Entrepreneurship Department and executive director of the Center for Entrepreneurship and Innovation at Grove City College. Mark Hendrickson is adjunct professor of economics and Fellow for Economic & Social Policy with the Center for Vision & Values at Grove City College. He is a contributor to Forbes.com, and sits on the Council of Scholars of the Commonwealth Foundation in Pennsylvania.

Brick Tower Press
Habent Sua Fata Libelli

Brick Tower Press
POB 342, Manhanset House
Shelter Island Hts., NY 11965-0342
bricktower@aol.com
www.BrickTowerPress.com

About the Book

"Let's get the consumer in the game. The idea behind HSAs is a 'supercharged IRA' for health care...No other program is as tax advantaged."
–John W. Snow, Treasury Secretary

"...HSAs can drastically lower an employer's costs of providing employee health benefits. This may allow more small businesses to offer such benefits."
–Fed Brock, The New York Times

"These accounts give workers the security of insurance against major illness, the opportunity to save tax-free for routine health expenses, and the freedom of knowing you can take your account with you whenever you change jobs."
–President George W. Bush

"Laing's new book (The Small Business Guide to HSAs) lives up to its name...an excellent explanation of how HSAs work..."
–Greg Scandlen, The New York Post

The Consumer's Guide to HSAs answers the question "What's in it for Me?" But responsibility doesn't stop there. You must read your medical reports, check statements, and count your pills carefully. Ask questions. Keep records for future use, and soon you will realize as much of the benefits of consumer-driven health care and HSAs as possible.

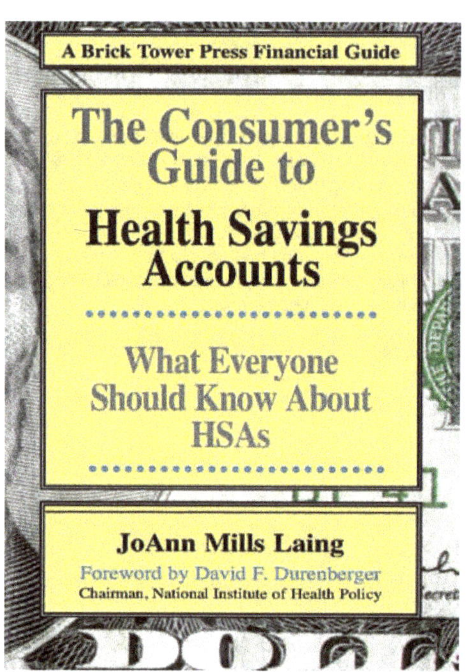

The Consumer's Guide to Health Savings Accounts
by JoAnn Mills Laing

Business & Economics : Finance

Print price $16.95
204 Pages
ISBN: 9781883283469
Binding: B&W 5.5 x 8.5 in or 216 x 140 mm (Demy 8vo) Perfect Bound on White w/Matte Lam

JoAnn M. Laing has 20+ years of experience envisioning, building and leveraging digital media, technology and information to increase sales, market share and profitability advising small businesses on how to grow. Ms. Laing is skilled in digital and multi-channel marketing. She was named a top woman in Silicon Alley and included in Folio's Top Women in Digital Media.

Brick Tower Press

Habent Sua Fata Libelli

Brick Tower Press
POB 342, Manhanset House
Shelter Island Hts., NY 11965-0342
bricktower@aol.com
www.BrickTowerPress.com

About the Book

"Skyrm makes complex financial scenarios accessible to all interested readers in an informative and entertaining manner. We can all learn something from this book." –Thomas Peterffy, Chairman, CEO, and President of Interactive Brokers

"Skyrm put together the story of MF Global like no one else could in providing the ultimate autopsy covering destructive financial engineering that's played such a big role in our capital markets." –Lawrence G. McDonald, New York Times best selling author of A COLOSSAL FAILURE OF COMMON SENSE

"God is in the details...first come the reporters, then the lawyers. Skyrm's book is the necessary antidote. Only someone who has 'done' it can explain it. Perhaps the best 'counterfactual' rationale for reading The Money Noose: If John Corzine had been able to before, there would likely have been no after." –Stan Jonas, Managing Partner, Axiom Management Partners

In 2010, President Barack Obama signed into law the Dodd-Frank Wall Street Reform and Consumer Protection Act. MF Global was bankrupt less than a year after the law's passage.

THE MONEY NOOSE is a general accounting of the facts that led to MF Global's collapse, as well as the story of the major players involved. It is a chaotic story, one in which individual actions taken in and of themselves are relatively minor. But the sum of those individual actions equal the same end result.

This book is designed to tell the story of MF Global, what went wrong and how things came to an abrupt end. In those regards, it's an incredible story.

The Money Noose: Jon Corzine and the Collapse of MF Global
by Scott E.D. Skyrm

Business & Economics : Finance
Business & Economics : Corporate & Business History

Print price $21.95
250 Pages
ISBN: 9781883283353
Binding: B&W 6 x 9 in or 229 x 152 mm Perfect Bound on White w/Gloss Lam

Scott E.D. Skyrm is one of the leading figures in the repo and securities finance markets today, and regularly quoted in The Wall Street Journal, The Financial Times, Bloomberg News Service, Reuters, Market News, and Dow Jones.

He is highly regarded as a former salesman, trader, trading desk manager, and global business head in fixed-income, securities finance, and securities clearing and settlement. He recently left Newedge, where he was their "Global Head of Repo, Money Markets, and Fixed Income Clearing."

Brick Tower Press

Habent Sua Fata Libelli

Brick Tower Press
POB 342, Manhanset House
Shelter Island Hts., NY 11965-0342
bricktower@aol.com
www.BrickTowerPress.com

About the Book

The aftershocks of the 2008 financial crisis still appear in the headlines most recently the government's quest to crush Moodys and S&P for failure to rate securities correctly given the risk. Were these agencies the only responsible parties?

"To me, as a multi-decade, veteran Lehman investment banker, the breathtaking death of my firm appeared impossible as little as three days ahead of the bankruptcy filing. Not only did I consider our 'master of the universe' firm invincible, but, like my colleagues, when it became clear we were in deep trouble, it was unfathomable that the US government could misstep so foolishly as to let any bulge bracket investment bank simply fail. The worst case seemed to be the Bear Stearns route."

For the first time, Joe Tibman pulls back the kimono to share intriguing information and detail about Lehman Brothers and the economic meltdown that has never before been revealed:

• How Lehman Brothers almost went under 10 years earlier but was, in a lucky turn of events, rescued from the brink of disaster when the U.S. government bailed out Mexico before it defaulted on billions of dollars in bonds?

• How, in the most detailed and intimate account of Lehman after the September 11, 2001 terrorist attack, when the firm and its people were ripped from their home, Fuld's "One Firm" strategy finally took root, sweeping away the vestiges of internal war inside Lehman's own halls, turning tragedy to triumph for a newly united firm where survival and success meant much more than a payday?

• What role did Paulson play? Cox? Bernanke? Greenspan? Geithner? Clinton? Phil Gramm? Congress? Summers?

• No reporter has ever been able to uncover why the rating agencies rated subprime securities so high. These agencies have never come clean with a clear statement on this issue. They just fired subprime analysts. For the first time in this book, Tibman discloses the key facts behind the subprime rating disaster.

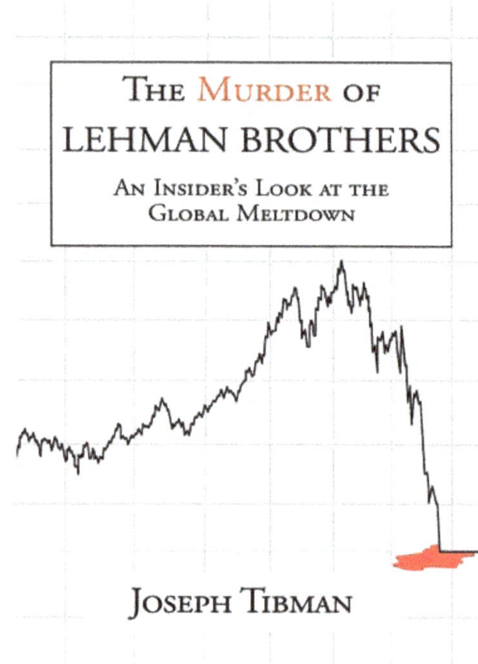

The Murder of Lehman Brothers, an Insider's Look at the Global Meltdown
by Joseph Tibman

The author worked in finance, both in commercial and investment banking for decades. For most of his career he was employed by the now bankrupt Lehman Brothers, where, over the years, as a senior investment banker, he held several positions. Like many Lehman colleagues, he holds undergraduate and graduate degrees from two highly regarded, elite universities.

Business & Economics : Finance
Business & Economics : Finance
Business & Economics : Corporate & Business History
Print price $21.95
254 Pages
ISBN: 9781883283223
Binding: B&W 6 x 9 in or 229 x 152 mm Perfect Bound on Creme w/Gloss Lam

Brick Tower Press
Habent Sua Fata Libelli

Brick Tower Press
POB 342, Manhanset House
Shelter Island Hts., NY 11965-0342
bricktower@aol.com
www.BrickTowerPress.com

About the Book

This is a true story of personal greed and downfall, corporate greed fueled with economic and social treachery, shareholder waste and discrimination at AIG, 70 Pine Street in the heart of the financial district. This address is know as the AIG Tower, hence our working title *** TOWER OF THIEVES ***

The central character is a man with a wife, a family, who has cheated his way to the top BY DOING GOOD. What he sees and what he does validates what unchecked power on Wall Street will do to a man and what it has done to an entire company and country. The events at AIG lead right to the CEO and Senior Vice Chairman and how our guy fights an entire corrupt organization and how he became one of those he despised.

"We found each other pretty easily - he recognized me from a photo that had appeared in the local paper about the book I was writing about Bear Stearns - and he asked if we could go 'somewhere more private' to talk. Part of me thought this was ridiculous. A big part of me, in fact. All this cloak-and-dagger nonsense seemed out of place in early summer Nantucket, Massachusetts, of all places. But there was some little sliver inside that told me this could be good. So I went along with it. We went to a park, sat down and, once we'd gotten through the formalities about how the Bear book was going, we got down to business. 'I should tell you that I'm going to federal prison at the end of the year,' he began.

"In my admittedly limited experience with such introductions, I have to say that any time a conversation starts with someone's announcing their impending sentencing date, fasten your seatbelt, because the story that follows is usually related to the sentencing date itself and is also usually pretty interesting. I took notes as John rolled out his story, the same story you're about to read here. After about five minutes, though, I realized I was no longer writing. I was just listening in disbelief to what he was telling me. This meeting took place long before AIG was the poster child for corporate greed and chutzpah. For that matter, this was before a lot of people had ever even heard of AIG, and even fewer people knew what they did as a corporation."

This is a story of what our taxpayer dollars have purchased.

Tower of Thieves, AIG
by Andrew Spencer

Business & Economics : Finance
Business & Economics : Finance
Business & Economics : Corporate & Business History
Print price $38.95
258 Pages
ISBN: 9781883283698
Binding: B&W 6.14 x 9.21 in or 234 x 156mm (Royal 8vo) Blue Cloth w/Jacket on White w/Gloss Lam

Andrew Spencer, the author of BEAR TRAP: THE FALL OF BEAR STEARNS AND THE PANIC OF 2008 and TOWER OF THIEVES: INSIDE AIG'S CORPORATE CULTURE OF GREED has been a summer resident of Nantucket for forty-one years, including ten years spent living on the island year-round. Today he lives with his wife Niki in Richmond, Virginia, and still enjoys spending summers on Nantucket.

Brick Tower Press

Habent Sua Fata Libelli

Brick Tower Press
POB 342, Manhanset House
Shelter Island Hts., NY 11965-0342
bricktower@aol.com
www.BrickTowerPress.com

About the Book

"Regardless of how respected or careful a company is, preparing for the possibility of a crisis is essential in today's business world. WHERE'S MY UMBRELLA offers valuable insights that any business should want to hear and follow."

Gary Sheffer
Vice President of Communications and Public Affairs.
GE

"The best way for any executive to manage any issue is to do so with a 360 view and to reach out to experts. There is no doubt that Len is someone to consult for expert advice."

Rick Sasso
President
MSC Cruises

Len, president of the communications counseling firm The Biegel Group brings his deep experience in a wide range of crises and reputation challenges to WHERE'S MY UMBRELLA. From the Tylenol tampering to 9/11 to hurricanes and environmental crimes, Biegel not only chronicles a host of wakeup calls. He tells what they mean. Len makes the case that many crises can be prevented.

Where's My Umbrella?

A Crash Course in
Crisis Management

LEN BIEGEL

UPDATED WITH LATEST CRISIS NEWS,
INCLUDING HURRICANE SANDY AND IMPACT ON BUSINESS.

Where's My Umbrella, a Crash Course in Crisis Management
by Len Biegel

Business & Economics : Insurance/Risk Assessment & Management

Print price $15.95
166 Pages
ISBN: 9781883283902
Binding: B&W 6 x 9 in or 229 x 152 mm Perfect Bound on White w/Matte Lam

Len Biegel's client list has included General Electric, American Airlines, Hershey Foods, The Business Roundtable, the Israel Broadcasting Authority, the North Atlantic Treaty Organization (NATO) - and a 20-year relationship with Royal Caribbean Cruises. He was formerly Senior Consultant for Fleishman Hillard, the head of the global crisis practice for Weber Shandwick and a senior executive with Burson Marsteller. An Emmy-winning television broadcaster, Len is a Senior Visiting Fellow with the Center for Risk Communication.

Brick Tower Press
Habent Sua Fata Libelli

Brick Tower Press
POB 342, Manhanset House
Shelter Island Hts., NY 11965-0342
bricktower@aol.com
www.BrickTowerPress.com

About the Book

What is the inside behind-the scenes story of Indian Casinos? More money than Las Vegas, more visitors than Disney World, and operating as sovereign nations exempt from all state civil law and many criminal laws; what is the"inside scoop"?

This is the only authoritative exploration of these multi-billion dollar enterprises; written by a genuine insider: the casino "guru" who has developed, operated, managed, and marketed Indian casinos all over the country. With unprecedented access to and cooperation from Tribes, the casinos, the staffs, the regulators, the lawyers, and the financers, the author (see "About the Author") is also an award-winning newspaper journalist with the writing credentials (and chops) to clearly present the subject.

With insider information, clear explanations, participation from Tribal officials, and authoritative revelations, the book is presented in story-progression form of how Indian casinos collectively generated more revenue last year than Microsoft and Google combined.

Osceola's Revenge: The Phenomena of Indian Casinos
by Gary Green

BUSINESS & ECONOMICS / Nonprofit Organizations & Charities / Finance & Accoun
History : Native American
Biography & Autobiography : Native Americans
Print price $29.95
206 Pages
ISBN: 9781899694723
Binding: B&W 6.00 x 9.00 in or 229 x 152mm (Royal 8vo) Blue Cloth w/Jacket on White w/Gloss Lam

GARY GREEN is one of the most written-about figures in modern casino circles. A former Donald Trump Vice President of Marketing and Player Development, he is a leading casino developer as well as the operational mastermind behind some of the most successful casinos in the country. He has been a leader in Native American (Indian) gaming since its inception and is a recurring speaker at trade shows in both Indian and commercial gaming. Beyond decades of stellar casino credentials and accolades in Indian Country, he is an award-winning former newspaper journalist (with more than a thousand by-lines) and twice nominated for the Pulitzer Prize for investigative reporting.

Brick Tower Press
Habent Sua Fata Libelli

Brick Tower Press
POB 342, Manhanset House
Shelter Island Hts., NY 11965-0342
bricktower@aol.com
www.BrickTowerPress.com

About the Book

For the first time, Liz Clark prepares elegant but simple bread recipes from her cooking school in Keokuk, Iowa. The recipes are prepared using wholesome ingredients, traditional bread making techniques with step-by-step instructions–and modern instructions for those of us who love our bread-making machines.

A full description about stone-ground flours found in your local supermarket and those flours found in small mills is included to round out our bread-making education not to mention a short history of these small mills where we can shop for flour with no additives or preservatives. Herbed Loaves, Black Olive & Walnut Bread with Thyme, Rosemary/Currant Bread, and Raison/Sunflower Seed Rye Loaf are just a few of the more than 50 bread recipes in the book. FRESH BREAD COMPANION was a featured title for BEA's Cookbook Expo 2001 in Chicago.

Fresh Bread Companion
by Liz Clark

Library: Companion
Cooking : Courses & Dishes/Bread

Print price $11.95
114 Pages
ISBN: 9781883283117
Binding: B&W 8.0 x 8.0 in or 203 x 203mm Perfect Bound on White w/Gloss Lam

The American Institute of Wine and Food featured Liz as one of the "Leading Chef's of the Mid West" in 1989. Author of many cookbooks including FRESH BREAD COMPANION, Liz co-authored APPLE COMPANION and contributed to the James Beard Foundation's THE JAMES BEARD CELEBRATION, edited by Barbara Kafka.

Brick Tower Press

Habent Sua Fata Libelli

Brick Tower Press
POB 342, Manhanset House
Shelter Island Hts., NY 11965-0342
bricktower@aol.com
www.BrickTowerPress.com

About the Book

SOUPS, STEWS, AND CHOWDERS bring credibility to the idea that America is a great melting pot. Philadelphia Pepper Pot Soup has its origins in George Washington's kitchen at Valley Forge during the winter encampment. Pigeon Soup was a particular favorite of Thomas Jefferson as pigeons were plentiful around Monticello. In colonial kitchens the predominate utensil was a large kettle. Cooks throughout the centuries have utilized whatever food was available to prepare delicious, invigorating, and warming soups for their families.

Sheilah Kaufman assembles over 70 soup recipes including Dill Pickle Soup, Pumpkin Mushroom Soup, Corn Chowder, and Clam Chowder to satisfy your nutritional urges. Some soups are hot and some are cold, but each recipe is elegant yet simple to prepare with easy clean-up.

Also included is a concise history of soups, stocks, and broths, notes about the origin of the terms we use today, and helpful hints to make your soup the envy of your neighborhood.

Soups, Stews and Chowders
by Sheilah Kaufman

Library: Companion
Cooking : Courses & Dishes/Soups & Stews

Print price $9.95
98 Pages
ISBN: 9781883283155
Binding: B&W 8.0 x 8.0 in or 203 x 203mm Perfect Bound on White w/Gloss Lam

Teachers from La Varenne in Paris and Le Cordon Bleu gave Sheilah her formal training in French cuisine. In 1966 Sheilah began teaching international cooking classes under the name French Cuisine Plus. Sheilah is the author of more than sixteen cookbooks including her bestselling FRENCH CUISINE PLUS, MORE FRENCH CUISINE PLUS, A CHICKEN IN EVERY POT, EASY WAYS TO ELEGANT COOKING, AND SHEILAH'S FEARLESS, FUSSLESS COOKING. Glamour magazine says "If you like to entertain, Sheilah's FEARLESS FUSSLESS COOKBOOK should be your best friend."

Brick Tower Press
Habent Sua Fata Libelli

Brick Tower Press
POB 342, Manhanset House
Shelter Island Hts., NY 11965-0342
bricktower@aol.com
www.BrickTowerPress.com

About the Book

I have met and worked with many entertainers in my life. The idea of this book came to me one evening while visiting Cuba. I expand on this in the chapter 'Finding a seed inside Havana.' Also, the wonderful actress Doris Roberts came for dinner one evening and wrote a letter that stated, "An extraordinary cook who takes pleasure in inviting his friends to his home for an evening of great food, wine and interesting conversation. The table is so beautiful that you hate to sit down to mess it up. The food that he cooks takes time, thoughtfulness and knowledge and he spends hours preparing it. Did I mention the aroma that greets you when you walk into his house?"

Seducing Celebrities One Meal at a Time
by Thaao Phenglis

Cooking : Entertaining
Biography & Autobiography : Rich & Famous
Biography & Autobiography : Entertainment & Performing Arts - General
Print price $34.95
224 Pages
ISBN: 9781899694570
Binding: Standard Color 6 x 9 in or 229 x 152 mm Blue Cloth w/Jacket on Standard 70 White w/Gloss Lam

Emmy nominated actor Thaao Penghlis was born and raised in Sydney, Australia to Greek-born parents. In 2015, Thaao was contracted to resume his most enduring character for NBC in Days of Our Lives, and then went on to star in the films Slow Dancing in the Big City, Altered States, The Mirror and The Bell Jar. Daytime audiences were first introduced to Penghlis in General Hospital. He also starred in the primetime series revival of Mission Impossible, which went on to be one of the most successful film franchises in history, with Tom Cruise. He starred in the mini-series Sadat, with Omar Sharif in Memories of Midnight and starred in the critically acclaimed television film Under Siege with Hal Holbrook for NBC. When he is off the stage, he is an intrepid world traveler, a gifted chef and a master storyteller.

Brick Tower Press

Habent Sua Fata Libelli

Brick Tower Press
POB 342, Manhanset House
Shelter Island Hts., NY 11965-0342
bricktower@aol.com
www.BrickTowerPress.com

About the Book
Thanksgiving Day!

What a wealth of images are evoked by this All-American holiday; a multitude of comforting sentiments that would require an American Dickens to do them justice.

Valiant be-buckled Pilgrims and their dignified Indian neighbors sit down to dinner in the serenity of an eternal golden autumn afternoon.

Radiant white churches welcome cheerful congregations from their rural homesteads supplying the bounty of the harvest. High school and college football teams defend their scholastic honor as preceding generations had under crisp blue autumn skies sensuously spiced with the faint aroma of burning leaves.

Generations converge on old New England homesteads where white-haired grandparents welcome the youngest members of the clan. Shocks of corn and heaps of pumpkins dot the fields and fill the barns, and the strutting monarch of the farmyard, the fattened Thanksgiving turkey, marches to his unsuspected fate. Pies are drawn steaming from cast-iron stoves on which bubbling pots foretell the forthcoming feast.

All of this would be recognized by generations of Americans as the essence of Thanksgiving.

Thanksgiving Cookery (8x10)
by Elizabeth Brabb, James W. Baker

Library: Companion
Cooking : Holiday
Cooking : History

Print price $14.95
98 Pages
ISBN: 9781883283032
Binding: B&W 8 x 10 in or 254 x 203mm Perfect Bound on White w/Gloss Lam

Elizabeth Brabb is the author of the first title in this series, AMERICAN CHEF'S COMPANION. Ms. Brabb's research in culinary styles resulted in this compilation of modern Thanksgiving recipes gathered from all parts of the country. A graduate of Skidmore College in Saratoga Springs, New York, she divides her time between Manhattan and Shelter Island where she lives with her husband and two children.

Jim spent years learning period cuisine and becoming a practiced antiquarian cook while librarian of Plimoth Plantation, overseeing the preparation of feasts for groups such as the Plantation Trustees, the Culinary Historians of Boston, and a period Thanksgiving for Julia Child on ABC TV. He is now Curator for the Alden House Historic Site in nearby Duxbury.

Brick Tower Press

Habent Sua Fata Libelli

Brick Tower Press
POB 342, Manhanset House
Shelter Island Hts., NY 11965-0342
bricktower@aol.com
www.BrickTowerPress.com

About the Book

This title jumps into the Christmas feast by spotlighting the tastes and fragrances of the American holiday.

From Oyster Soup and Parsley Sauce to Currant Jelly and Yule Dollies, the book explores recipes and cooking ideas popular in the 19th century, but with the palate of the modern family in focus. If you'd like to know how the tradition of Christmas dinner started and sample some true American favorites, then this book is a must for your kitchen library.

Easy to read with clear step-by-step directions, don't miss it this season.

Victorian Christmas Cookery
by Bruce T. Paddock

Library: Companion
Cooking : Holiday

Print price $11.95
98 Pages
ISBN: 9781883283063
Binding: B&W 8.0 x 8.0 in or 203 x 203mm Perfect Bound on White w/Gloss Lam

Bruce T. Paddock has been involved with the past for almost as long as he's been alive in the present. This interest led him to get a degree in History from Yale University. While living in Los Angeles, at both the Doctor's House (a restored Victorian house) and the Heritage Square Museum (a restored Victorian Village) as a lecturer, interpreter, and historical researcher. Bruce has been an afficionado of food for nearly as long. Of course, experience is useless without the ability to communicate it, and Bruce has over twenty years of experience in non-fiction writing. He and his family live in Connecticut.

Brick Tower Press

Habent Sua Fata Libelli

Brick Tower Press
POB 342, Manhanset House
Shelter Island Hts., NY 11965-0342
bricktower@aol.com
www.BrickTowerPress.com

About the Book

"Clark creates many of the down-home recipes of her farm childhood." -The Des Moines Register.

Each luscious apple recipe was created by one of the best known culinary professionals in the Midwest–Liz Clark. In an Italinate, Villa-Style house, above the Mississippi River in Keokuk, Iowa, Liz prepared each recipe described in this book from Tailgate Pea Soup with Apples to Chicken Liver Paté with Apples.

Recently reviewed in the Des Moines Register, this book will become a classic American cookbook. If the recipes aren't enough to grab your palate, Jill Vorbeck's enlightening story about apples will certainly get your attention. Listing many examples of apple varieties, some known, and others not known, Jill talks about preparing apples for Liz's delightful recipes.

You will understand the best way to peel, core, and slice apples quickly as well as know what kinds of apples you can use. We guarantee Jill will assist even the most experienced cook in the preparation of apples.

Apple Companion
by Liz Clark

Library: Companion
Cooking : Specific Ingredients - Fruit

Print price $11.95
114 Pages
ISBN: 9781883283056
Binding: B&W 8.0 x 8.0 in or 203 x 203mm Perfect Bound on White w/Gloss Lam

The American Institute of Wine and Food featured Liz as one of the "Leading Chef's of the Mid West" in 1989. Author of many cookbooks including FRESH BREAD COMPANION, Liz co-authored APPLE COMPANION and contributed to the James Beard Foundation's THE JAMES BEARD CELEBRATION, edited by Barbara Kafka.

Jill Vorbeck, the "apple lady," peels, cores, and slices apples in a farm kitchen in central Illinois. Jill and her husband grow over 200 varieties of apples and operate Applesource– the mail order marketplace for specialty apples.

Brick Tower Press
POB 342, Manhanset House
Shelter Island Hts., NY 11965-0342
bricktower@aol.com
www.BrickTowerPress.com

Brick Tower Press

Habent Sua Fata Libelli

About the Book

"Clark and Baker have brought out a charming, informative cookbook with wonderful recipes,"
–Janeen Sarlin, The Southampton Press

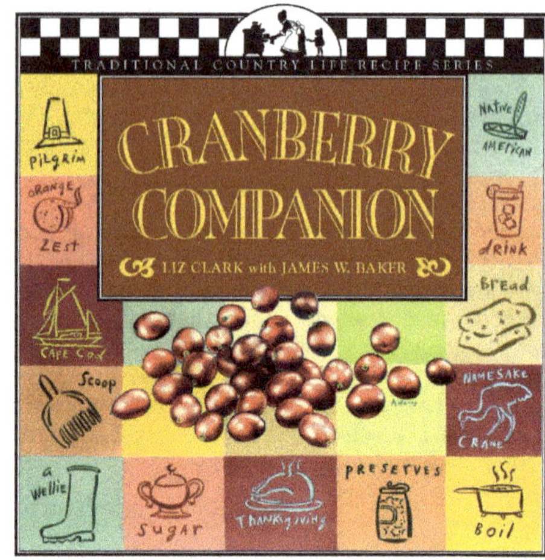

James Baker contributes a detailed and well-organized story about cranberries from the pre-colonial period to the present day. Liz Clark's marvelous and mouthwatering recipes will alert everyone to the nutritional and culinary value of the cranberry.

Cranberries are more American than apple pie. It wouldn't be Thanksgiving without cranberry sauce, and Christmas dinner in America would be incomplete without the traditional cranberry condiment. Yet while the Pilgrims undoubtedly brought a memory of apple pie (and apple pie memories were all they had in 1621) to the "First Thanksgiving," they weren't having similar thoughts about cranberry sauce. Neither written nor oral tradition can enlighten us whether the berries played any role at all in that famous three-day feast in 1621, and if they did, it wasn't in the form of our familiar sweet sauce.

Cranberries have played a supporting role in American cuisine for so long that we take the familiar dark red fruit for granted, vaguely assuming that they were eaten from the time Plymouth Rock was still news. However, unlike the starring roles enjoyed by corn, pumpkins and turkeys in the colonial records, cranberries humbly avoided the spotlight of history. They crept into colonial life unheralded, and appear incidentally in early records with no mention as to their first discovery or use.

Cranberry Companion was a featured title for BEA's Cookbook Expo.

Cranberry Companion
by Liz Clark

Library: Companion
Cooking : Specific Ingredients - Fruit
Cooking : History

Print price $11.95
116 Pages
ISBN: 9781883283285
Binding: B&W 8.0 x 8.0 in or 203 x 203mm Perfect Bound on White w/Gloss Lam

The American Institute of Wine and Food featured Liz as one of the "Leading Chef's of the Mid West" in 1989. Author of many cookbooks including FRESH BREAD COMPANION, Liz co-authored APPLE COMPANION and contributed to the James Beard Foundation's THE JAMES BEARD CELEBRATION, edited by Barbara Kafka.

After his appointment as Director of Research at Plimoth Plantation in 1978, James Baker helped design the Plantation's critically acclaimed first-person role playing program. Mr. Baker's research with pilgrim period recipes helped him prepare an accurate "First Thanksgiving" dinner for Julia Child on "Good Morning America" in 1983.

Brick Tower Press
Habent Sua Fata Libelli

Brick Tower Press
POB 342, Manhanset House
Shelter Island Hts., NY 11965-0342
bricktower@aol.com
www.BrickTowerPress.com

About the Book

Morton and Preston, both experienced herb gardeners, present a unique collection of recipes suited for every palate. This collection uses commonly grown and easily accessible garden herbs found throughout American folklore from the Pilgrims to modern times. In 1796, Amelia Simmons wrote, in the First American Cookbook, "Garlicks, tho' used by the French, are better adapted to the use of medicine than cooking." How tastes have changed in 200 years! From Sage and Raisin Scones to Zucchini Pickles, every herb has its day.

Fresh Herb Companion
by Jane Morton, Marianne K. Preston

Library: Companion
Cooking : Specific Ingredients - Fruit
Cooking : History

Print price $11.95
98 Pages
ISBN: 9781883283049
Binding: B&W 8.0 x 8.0 in or 203 x 203mm Perfect Bound on White w/Gloss Lam

Jane Wilson Morton has been cultivating and cooking with fresh herbs for over 30 years. She studied with Giuliano Bugialli in Italy, Simone Beck in France, Bruno Ellmer at the Culinary Institute of America in Hyde Park, New York, and others in New York City, California, and Thailand. Jane attended Skidmore College and holds BA and MS degrees from Queens College, New York.

Marianne K. Preston was a cooking instructor, food writer, and restaurant reviewer. She was a proprietor of a gourmet shop, The Amateur Gourmet, from 1974 to 1978, and then went on to teach and to write about food for many publications. Her food column byline was Cuisine Avec Panache.

Brick Tower Press
Habent Sua Fata Libelli

Brick Tower Press
POB 342, Manhanset House
Shelter Island Hts., NY 11965-0342
bricktower@aol.com
www.BrickTowerPress.com

About the Book

The trouble is we don't know who made that first dish of vanilla, strawberry or triple chocolate chunk ice cream. That may explain why there are candidates for the honor all over the world. Some give the ancient Romans credit for inventing ice cream, but although they did send their slaves off to the mountains to get snow, they didn't make ice cream with it. They poured syrup on it and ate it, or they used it to chill their wines or fruit.

At the turn of the twenty-first century, Americans were eating 23 quarts of ice cream per person, per year, more than any other country. Vanilla was America's favorite flavor, with chocolate coming in second. The health issues associated with ice cream were no longer colic and cold stomachs; they were fat and cholesterol. Nevertheless, premium and super-premium ice cream sales were growing, and low-fat ice cream sales were shrinking. Manufacturers were researching the possibility of adding Omega-3 fatty acids to ice cream to give it the health benefits associated with salmon.

With all the premium ice creams on the market today, why make your own? Because it's easy and it's fun. You don't need ice and salt for today's ice cream makers, and they're affordable and simple to use. You control the ingredients so you know exactly what's in your ice cream. No guar gum or salmon required. You can use your imagination, experiment with flavors and add your own chunky bits. You, like me, can make ice cream that's parfaite.

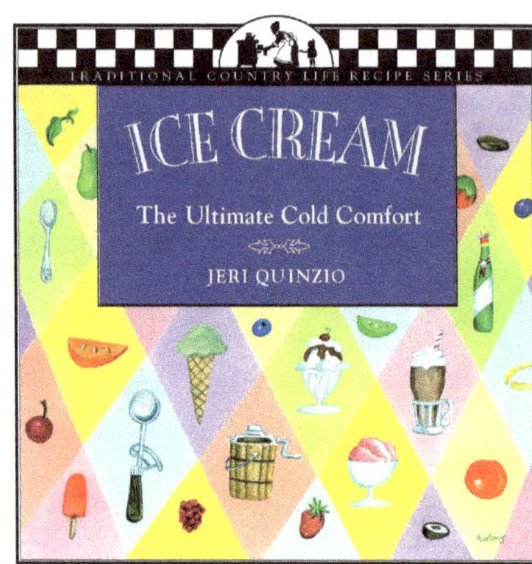

Ice Cream: The Ultimate Cold Comfort
by Jeri Quinzo

Jeri Quinzio is a freelance writer and past president of the Culinary Historians of Boston. Jeri has contributed to the Radcliffe Culinary Times and Gastronomica.

Library: Companion
Cooking : Specific Ingredients - General

Print price $11.95
114 Pages
ISBN: 9781883283360
Binding: B&W 8.0 x 8.0 in or 203 x 203mm Perfect Bound on White w/Gloss Lam

Brick Tower Press

Habent Sua Fata Libelli

Brick Tower Press
POB 342, Manhanset House
Shelter Island Hts., NY 11965-0342
bricktower@aol.com
www.BrickTowerPress.com

About the Book

We would like to think that this farmstand vegetable cookbook will encourage you to seek out a farmstand in your own home town and, when traveling in a rural or urban area, to stop at a farmstand or greenmarket. Take time to talk to the stand owner, learn about the different varieties of vegetables he offers and how to prepare them. You might just find yourself chatting with the produce grower, gaining useful information about the produce you are buying and then even sharing a recipe or two. Enjoy the ambiance of the farmstand and give a thought to the needs, the toil and the entrepreneurship that brought the legendary farmstand to the position it holds today, for it is a small but very integral part of our American history.

The recipes in this book will inspire you not only to "eat your veggies" but to "love your veggies."

Farmstand Companion
by Jane Morton, Marianne K. Preston

Library: Companion
Cooking : Specific Ingredients - Natural Foods
Cooking : History
Gardening : Vegetables
Print price $12.95
112 Pages
ISBN: 9781883283213
Binding: B&W 8.0 x 8.0 in or 203 x 203mm Perfect Bound on White w/Gloss Lam

Jane Wilson Morton has been cultivating and cooking with fresh herbs for over 30 years. She studied with Giuliano Bugialli in Italy, Simone Beck in France, Bruno Ellmer at the Culinary Institute of America in Hyde Park, New York, and others in New York City, California, and Thailand. Jane attended Skidmore College and holds BA and MS degrees from Queens College, New York.

Marianne K. Preston was a cooking instructor, food writer, and restaurant reviewer. She was a proprietor of a gourmet shop, The Amateur Gourmet, from 1974 to 1978, and then went on to teach and to write about food for many publications. Her food column byline was Cuisine Avec Panache.

Brick Tower Press
POB 342, Manhanset House
Shelter Island Hts., NY 11965-0342
bricktower@aol.com
www.BrickTowerPress.com

Brick Tower Press

Habent Sua Fata Libelli

About the Book

During their prime season, zucchini seem to spring up overnight. What wasn't there yesterday is ready for picking at dawn today. They grow with such abandon that on a dewy morning one might well scream, "Heaven's to Betsy, what am I supposed to do with them?" Pick them, my dear, at once. And enjoy them.

Elizabeth David, the celebrated British gastronomic writer, championed the cause of baby zucchini so forcefully that growers actually bowed to her wishes. Her influence was equally felt by the public. In the Oxford Companion to Food, Alan Davidson wrote that zucchini "only became popular in England after Elizabeth David in the 1950s and l960s had introduced them to readers of her books."

Grow Your Own was the dictum of Jane Grigson, another British cookbook writer. "Even if you haven't a garden, you can buy a couple of zucchini plants from a nurseryman and grow them in the backyard or on a balcony in a tub. Until you have grown them yourself and picked them at 2-6 inches in length you cannot imagine how delicious they can be. Put them straight into the pan with a knob of butter and seasoning. Jam on the lid with foil and stew gently for about five minutes. That is all you should do with so perfect and fresh a vegetable."

Adorable Zucchini: More Magic Than the Pumpkin
by Naomi Barry

Library: Companion
Cooking : Specific Ingredients/Vegetables
Cooking : History

Print price $11.95
102 Pages
ISBN: 9781883283339
Binding: B&W 8.0 x 8.0 in or 203 x 203mm Perfect Bound on White w/Gloss Lam

Naomi Barry lives in Paris, spends part of each year in Italy and has written articles datelined from five continents, primarily for Gourmet and the International Herald Tribune. Books include Paris Personal, Paris à Table, Food alla Florentine and a forthcoming memoir of the world's greatest hotelier since Cesar Ritz.

Brick Tower Press

Habent Sua Fata Libelli

Brick Tower Press
POB 342, Manhanset House
Shelter Island Hts., NY 11965-0342
bricktower@aol.com
www.BrickTowerPress.com

About the Book

The Growing Menace–More and more, homeowners and gardeners throughout rural and suburban America have been forced to deal with a growing menace.... Deer!

From coast to coast, deer have developed quite an appetite for almost anything growing in our landscapes and gardens. Deer frequently feed on flowers, fruits, vegetables and the twigs of trees and shrubs, often permanently disfiguring them. In winter, bucks rub their antlers on sapling trees and shrubs, severely damaging the bark and seriously threatening the health and life of the plant. As a result, deer have become a big a nuisance to home gardeners and professionals who design and maintain landscapes and gardens.

The economic costs caused by deer browsing damage in the U.S. amounts to millions of dollars every year. Replacing plantings is one thing but even more is spent on repellents, fences and numerous other strategies for protecting landscapes, home gardens and agricultural crops from deer browsing damage. Suburban sprawl, increased abandoned farmlands and unchecked growing populations of deer are just some of the reasons deer have become such a costly nuisance around the country.

This book is to help and guide home gardeners and professionals with creating pleasing and colorful flowerbeds and borders in deer country by using deer resistant flowers and other plants. With a list of well over 350 flowers and ornamental plants, FLOWERBEDS AND BORDERS IN DEER COUNTRY will help you select plants that are known to have a resistance to deer browsing damage.

Flowerbeds and Borders in Deer Country: For the Home and Garden
by Vincent Drzewucki

Library: Deer Country
Gardening : Garden Design

Print price $11.95
108 Pages
ISBN: 9781883283292
Binding: B&W 8.0 x 8.0 in or 203 x 203mm Perfect Bound on White w/Gloss Lam

Vincent Drzewucki Jr. is a horticulturist, lecturer, and director of the Long Island Nurserymen's Association in New York State. He is a New York State Certified Nursery Professional, a New York State DEC Certified Commercial Pesticide Applicator, and a US private pilot. Advanced degrees include an AAS in Ornamental Horticulture and Nursery Management from SUNY Agriculture and Technical College, Farmingdale, New York, and an MBA from Adelphi University, Garden City, New York. Vincent lives with his wife in Wantaugh, New York.

Brick Tower Press

Habent Sua Fata Libelli

Brick Tower Press
POB 342, Manhanset House
Shelter Island Hts., NY 11965-0342
bricktower@aol.com
www.BrickTowerPress.com

About the Book

•"... a must-have for anyone who's tired of pouring heart and soul into landscaping the yard, only to have everything eaten by thieves in the night."
–Rural Heritage

•"Too bad I didn't own this book before selecting balsam. Balsams are rated 'F,' as in never plant em' near deer."
–Timothy Fay, Wapsipinicon Almanac

•"The information is presented in an easy-to-read format."
–Woman's Day

•"Gardening in Deer Country should find a large audience...you will find useful information in this book...."
–Bob Gibbs, Audubon Naturalist News

•"...worthwhile and practical..."
–NBC's TODAY Show

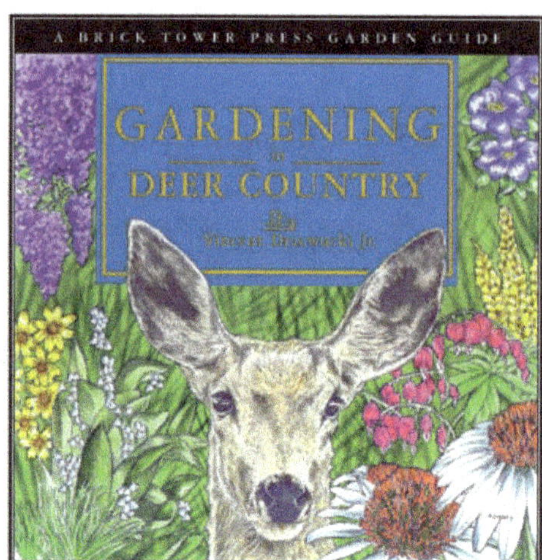

Deer...you love them or you hate them, but no matter what deer have an appetite for delicious plants we plant in our garden and around our home. You've seen the residue in the morning: spiked hostas, chomped impatiens, mangled hydrangea. How can an animal that cute be so hungry? Fences and sprays and dogs just don't go far enough and most people stop short of venison surprise for dinner. What's a serious gardener to do? GARDENING IN DEER COUNTRY answers this question by presenting descriptions of trees, shrubs, annuals, perennials, ground covers, herbs, bulbs, and vines that deer don't like to eat.

Gardening in Deer Country
by Vincent Drzewucki

Library: Deer Country
Gardening : Landscape

Print price $11.95
114 Pages
ISBN: 9781883283452
Binding: B&W 8.0 x 8.0 in or 203 x 203mm Perfect Bound on White w/Gloss Lam

Vincent Drzewucki Jr. is a horticulturist, lecturer, and director of the Long Island Nurserymen's Association in New York State. He is a New York State Certified Nursery Professional, a New York State DEC Certified Commercial Pesticide Applicator, and a US private pilot. Advanced degrees include an AAS in Ornamental Horticulture and Nursery Management from SUNY Agriculture and Technical College, Farmingdale, New York, and an MBA from Adelphi University, Garden City, New York. Vincent lives with his wife in Wantaugh, New York.

Brick Tower Press

Habent Sua Fata Libelli

Brick Tower Press
POB 342, Manhanset House
Shelter Island Hts., NY 11965-0342
bricktower@aol.com
www.BrickTowerPress.com

About the Book

•"... a must-have for anyone who's tired of pouring heart and soul into landscaping the yard, only to have everything eaten by thieves in the night."
–Rural Heritage

•"Too bad I didn't own this book before selecting balsam. Balsams are rated 'F,' as in never plant em' near deer."
–Timothy Fay, Wapsipinicon Almanac

•"The information is presented in an easy-to-read format."
–Woman's Day

•"Gardening in Deer Country should find a large audience...you will find useful information in this book...."
–Bob Gibbs, Audubon Naturalist News

•"...worthwhile and practical..."
–NBC's TODAY Show

Deer...you love them or you hate them, but no matter what deer have an appetite for delicious plants we plant in our garden and around our home. You've seen the residue in the morning: spiked hostas, chomped impatiens, mangled hydrangea. How can an animal that cute be so hungry? Fences and sprays and dogs just don't go far enough and most people stop short of venison surprise for dinner. What's a serious gardener to do? GARDENING IN DEER COUNTRY answers this question by presenting descriptions of trees, shrubs, annuals, perennials, ground covers, herbs, bulbs, and vines that deer don't like to eat.

Gardening in Deer Country: For the Home and Garden
by Vincent Drzewucki

Library: Deer Country
Gardening : Techniques

Print price $14.95
114 Pages
ISBN: 9781883283094
Binding: B&W 8 x 10 in or 254 x 203mm Perfect Bound on White w/Gloss Lam

Vincent Drzewucki Jr. is a horticulturist, lecturer, and director of the Long Island Nurserymen's Association in New York State. He is a New York State Certified Nursery Professional, a New York State DEC Certified Commercial Pesticide Applicator, and a US private pilot. Advanced degrees include an AAS in Ornamental Horticulture and Nursery Management from SUNY Agriculture and Technical College, Farmingdale, New York, and an MBA from Adelphi University, Garden City, New York. Vincent lives with his wife in Wantaugh, New York.

Brick Tower Press

Habent Sua Fata Libelli

Brick Tower Press
POB 342, Manhanset House
Shelter Island Hts., NY 11965-0342
bricktower@aol.com
www.BrickTowerPress.com

About the Book

"The Oxygen Plan was a life-changer simply because it put me in control of my choices, while giving me structure to define and categorize my issues."
–Lorraine Lucciola, freelance writer

Why Oxygen? Oxygen supports life.

The Oxygen Plan offers viable behavioral tools and professional support for abundant happiness, fulfillment and maximized potential, by exploring the foundations of stress, which are different for each of us, and by presenting new methods of managing it.

Our goal is to usher you into the green, by presenting a multi-faceted understanding of what being healthy–physically, emotionally, socially and behaviorally–feels like.

Optimism is its own self-fulfilling prophecy. Optimism embraces our hope, our strength and our perseverance. One positive thought or action engenders the next positive thought or action. Optimism is powerful and persuasive. It tells your brain that you can do great things. And you can.

The Oxygen Plan
by Eric Lucas

Health & Fitness : Healing

Print price $12.95
116 Pages
ISBN: 9781590190005
Binding: B&W 6 x 9 in or 229 x 152 mm Perfect Bound on White w/Gloss Lam

Author Eric Lucas, the founder and chief executive of The Oxygen Plan Corporation, is a marketing executive with a long track record of creating breakthrough innovations and leading them to success. Prior to creating and leading The Oxygen Plan, Lucas spent 22 years with General Mills, rising to the level of corporate officer, vice-president of marketing and head of New Ventures for the 31,000 employee Fortune 200 Company. He also led promotional campaigns for the 1996, 2000, and 2002 Olympic Games, Disney, NFL, NBA, and MLB for General Mills.

Brick Tower Press
Habent Sua Fata Libelli

Brick Tower Press
POB 342, Manhanset House
Shelter Island Hts., NY 11965-0342
bricktower@aol.com
www.BrickTowerPress.com

About the Book

This book offers a framework of science and experience to encourage both women and men to live a balanced life, and to help maintain wellness even in the face of stress and trouble. It also encourages you to ask questions, to examine facts, and to think before reacting in fear. This book contains advice based upon scientific evidence and explains the social and political environment shaping this information. Use it as a guide to help you make good decisions.

"What has been frustrating for me as a doctor, and I know for you as a patient, is that there is never enough time to ask questions and get the answers that you need and deserve. So think of this book as you read it, as our time together as doctor and patient, but in the comfort of your home."

Stellar Medicine, a Journey Through the Universe of Women's Health
by Saralyn Mark

Health & Fitness : Women's Health

Print price $19.95
256 Pages
ISBN: 9781883283780
Binding: B&W 6 x 9 in or 229 x 152 mm Perfect Bound on Creme w/Gloss Lam

Dr. Saralyn Mark is a world-renowned leader and pioneer in woman's health. An endocrinologist, geriatrician, and woman's health specialist, she was the first senior medical advisor to the Office on Women's Health within the Department of Health and Human Services and is a medical consulate for NASA.

She designed the first women's health fellowship in the U.S., helped create the National Centers of Leadership in Academic Medicine, the National Centers of Excellence in Women's Health, and landmark educational campaigns on critical health issues. Dr. Mark, a faculty member at Yale and other universities, has lectured around the world and is a frequent contributor to media outlets including CNN, Good Morning America Health, and the Washington Post.

As president of SolaMed Solutions, LLC, she

Brick Tower Press

Habent Sua Fata Libelli

Brick Tower Press
POB 342, Manhanset House
Shelter Island Hts., NY 11965-0342
bricktower@aol.com
www.BrickTowerPress.com

About the Book

"A respected historian and researcher" –Publishers Weekly

"A prize is waiting somewhere out there, which Linda Holmes richly deserves for revisiting some appalling realities in a positive way fifty years after the fact."
–Nancy Steffens Seaman, Smithsonian Magazine's Board of Editors

"A tribute to courage and determination of the men who endured it...I ate the book up, and was disappointed to come to the end so fast, and this hasn't happened to me in a long time." –Otto Schwarz, Burma Railway survivor and founder, USS Houston Survivors' Association.

"Linda Goetz Holmes has focused on a most interesting, and somewhat neglected, period of the Allied POW experience – the hiatus between the end of the war and the return home... A useful addition to the growing body of literature on the Allied POW experience in Asia."–Tim Bowden, Australian author and documentary producer.

During the early days of World War II, Cecil Dickson and much of the 2/2 Australian Pioneer Battalion were forced to surrender to the Japanese. This group of POWs, along with captured American National Guard soldiers from Texas and California, and survivors from the sunk USS Houston, were shipped to Burma and Thailand to construct the infamous "Railway of Death" immortalized in the film Bridge Over the River Kwai. 16,000 Allied POWs would die toiling on the railway, and those who lived endured over three years of harsh slave labor until they were released to journey home. Respected military historian Linda Goetz Holmes tells Dickson's story of his experiences in Japanese labor camps and his determined plan to survive and return to a normal life. Amazing photographs, taken secretly by other prisoners, and personal letters help chronicle this dark chapter in the history of Allied troops in the Pacific.

4000 Bowls of Rice: A Prisoner of War Comes Home
by Linda Goetz Holmes

History : Military - World War II

Print price $18.95
210 Pages
ISBN: 9781883283513
Binding: B&W 6 x 9 in or 229 x 152 mm Perfect Bound on Creme w/Gloss Lam

Linda Goetz Holmes is the first Pacific War historian appointed to the U.S. Government Nazi War Crimes and Japanese Imperial Government Records Interagency Working Group, tasked with locating and declassifying documents about World War II war crimes. A graduate of Wellesley College, she has been writing about Pacific prisoners of war for 30 years, and has been interviewed many times by national and local TV and radio stations, and appeared in documentaries on the History Channel, Fox News, and ABC 20/20, to name but a few. She is also the author of: UNJUST ENRICHMENT: HOW JAPAN'S COMPANIES BUILT POST-WAR FORTUNES USING AMERICAN POWS (2001) and a frequent speaker to veterans' groups.

Brick Tower Press

Habent Sua Fata Libelli

Brick Tower Press
POB 342, Manhanset House
Shelter Island Hts., NY 11965-0342
bricktower@aol.com
www.BrickTowerPress.com

About the Book

"This convoy must not get through-U-boats pursue, attack and sink."

This was the signal that Admiral Dönitz sent to the commanders of the 21 U-boats of the Markgraf wolf-pack on September 9, 1941 just before the United States entered the war.

Sixty-three merchant ships; a number old and dilapidated and all slow and heavy laden with vital supplies from the United States for the United Kingdom, were strung out in 12 columns abreast, covering 25 miles of inhospitable ocean. They set sail from Nova Scotia at a time when the German U-boats were sinking more than one hundred ships a month and the US Navy could do nothing but stand-by and watch-at least officially.

"Around noon, the three US destroyers, Charles F. Hughes, Russell and Sims, wheeled away and made off to the west at speed. The American ships had served their purpose, for although they had taken great pains not to be associated with SC42's official escort, the mere presence of these modern, powerful men-of-war had contributed to the withdrawal of the U-boats." The convoy's escort of one destroyer and three corvettes of the Royal Canadian Navy, all untried in combat, was hopelessly outclassed when the battle for SC42 commenced. The battle lasted for seven days and covered 1,200 miles of ocean. First hand accounts by participants on both sides add interest and drama.

Attack & Sink, the Battle of the Atlantic, Summer 1941
by Bernard Edwards

History : Military - World War II
World War II

Print price $15.95
228 Pages
ISBN: 9781899694402
Binding: B&W 6 x 9 in or 229 x 152 mm Perfect Bound on White w/Gloss Lam

With 37 years at sea under his belt, Captain Bernard Edwards has over ten titles in print including SOS-MEN AGAINST THE SEA, BLOOD & BUSHIDO, RETURN OF THE COFFIN SHIPS, AND SALVO! A resident of Wales, Captain Edwards is close to the sea he writes about. His lifetime experience at sea enables him to add authentic touches and bring official reports to life.

Brick Tower Press
POB 342, Manhanset House
Shelter Island Hts., NY 11965-0342
bricktower@aol.com
www.BrickTowerPress.com

About the Book

Imperial Japan's wartime atrocities left a bloody stain on the waters of the Pacific...

This is a story that might have quietly slipped beneath the waves of history had Bernard Edwards not written this important book. The book vividly recounts the barbaric actions of Japan's navy in the wake of its attacks on Allied shipping, including the ramming of lifeboats, the machine-gunning of survivors and the bayoneting and beheading of captives.

As Edwards explains, the ancient Japanese warrior code of Bushido – under which capture is forbidden– was in stark and lethal contrast to the humane code of conduct usually honored by seafarers. Anyone unfortunate enough to fall victim to the Imperial Navy paid a terrible price. Drawing on the dramatic accounts of Allied survivors, this book serves as a reminder of the Imperial Navy's inhumane acts and a tribute to those who perished because of them.

A selection of the Military Book Club.

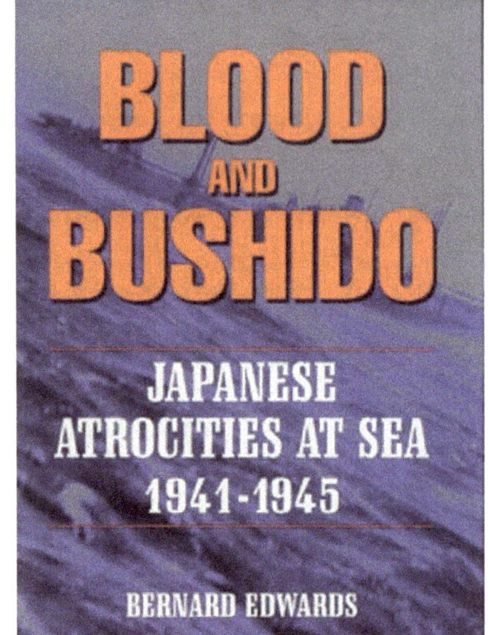

Blood And Bushido
by Bernard Edwards

History : Military - World War II

Print price $13.95
258 Pages
ISBN: 9781883283872
Binding: B&W 6 x 9 in or 229 x 152 mm Perfect Bound on Creme w/Gloss Lam

With 37 years at sea under his belt, Captain Bernard Edwards has over ten titles in print including SOS-MEN AGAINST THE SEA, BLOOD & BUSHIDO, RETURN OF THE COFFIN SHIPS, AND SALVO! A resident of Wales, Captain Edwards is close to the sea he writes about. His lifetime experience at sea enables him to add authentic touches and bring official reports to life.

Brick Tower Press

Habent Sua Fata Libelli

Brick Tower Press
POB 342, Manhanset House
Shelter Island Hts., NY 11965-0342
bricktower@aol.com
www.BrickTowerPress.com

About the Book

Here at last is the true story of the merchant fleet during World War II, the non-fighting service in which 32,000 men died yet whose essential role has never been fully appreciated. The author, himself a member of the service from 1941-47, relates the stories of merchantmen and their crews with unique insight. From the early days of the war to the day of victory on the Rhine, through combined operations in the Mediterranean and at Normandy, the complete operation of the fleet is examined, with vivid accounts of the horrific losses undergone, the heroism of the crews and the sacrifices endured to ensure that Britain received its essential supplies of food, oil, and raw materials. Highly illustrated, this book will be absorbing for the war historian, maritime enthusiast and general reader alike.

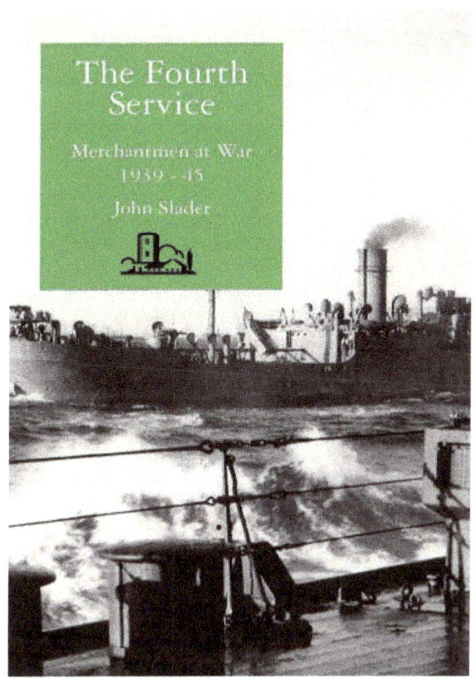

The Fourth Service
by John Slader

John Slader joined the merchant navy in 1941 at the age of 17. Within two years he had survived being torpedoed on two separate occasions. After the war, he worked as an import/export executive for 32 years. Since retiring he has been freelance writer, concentrating on maritime and county life subjects. THE FOURTH SERVICE is his sixth book.

History : Military - World War II

Print price $23.95
384 Pages
ISBN: 9781876963132
Binding: B&W 6 x 9 in or 229 x 152 mm Perfect Bound on Creme w/Gloss Lam

Brick Tower Press

Habent Sua Fata Libelli

Brick Tower Press
POB 342, Manhanset House
Shelter Island Hts., NY 11965-0342
bricktower@aol.com
www.BrickTowerPress.com

About the Book

"Let's keep in the bond."
–Leon Uris, bestselling author of EXODUS and TRINITY.

The Allied forces had been battling the Japanese Empire in the Pacific War since 1941, flattening island after island for three and a half years. Now, it was Okinawa's turn. The Japanese engineers had scarred the paradise by building three major airfields, affording a tempting morsel for the American juggernaut and a strategic entry point to Japan itself.

On April 1, 1945, ironically April Fool's Day and Easter Sunday, the invasion of Okinawa began. Thousands of warships and aircraft appeared, dumping tons of high explosives on the pristine little island. Tens of thousands of American infantrymen stormed their beaches. Within the flick of an eyelash the quaint little villages were reduced to rubble. The beautiful fields of rice and sugar cane looked as though a giant heavenly shotgun had blasted them into a quagmire of mud and broken debris.

Fortunately, the islanders were warned in advance to dig caves in the mountainsides where they could seek refuge. This they did, and this is where they hid for three months as the battle raged over their heads. For tactical reasons, the Japanese commander decided to make his stand in the south. Thus, the lower end of the island was demolished, leaving the north unscathed. Perhaps fate stepped in and decided to preserve at least half of this wonderful civilization. Many of the riflemen who survived the flames of combat in the south were sent north and allowed to mingle with these gracious people. This story belongs to them.

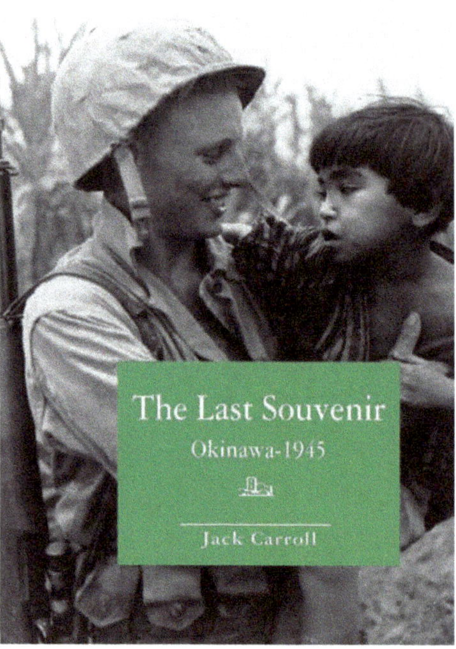

The Last Souvenir: Okinawa - 1945
by Jack Caroll

History : Military - World War II

Print price $16.95
446 Pages
ISBN: 9781876963040
Binding: B&W 5.5 x 8.5 in or 216 x 140 mm (Demy 8vo) Perfect Bound on White w/Gloss Lam

Jack Carroll enlisted in the United States Marine Corps in 1944, trained in Camp Pendleton, and later served under Chesty Puller. He served four years in the Marine Corps and was honorably discharged. His experiences were to both enlighten and haunt him for a lifetime. His "time in hell" was spent fighting the Japanese army during the islanding hopping campaign, then surviving Guadalcanal as a gunnery sargeant. His most horrific story was when an armed Japanese foot-soldier opted to blow himself up with a hand-granade, rather than risk capture. Jack returned to a job with Merrill Lynch after the war and lived in Southern Califonia with his wife, Mary, and two children, He died unexpectedly in 2000.

Brick Tower Press
Habent Sua Fata Libelli

Brick Tower Press
POB 342, Manhanset House
Shelter Island Hts., NY 11965-0342
bricktower@aol.com
www.BrickTowerPress.com

About the Book
"Eric Wiberg's ability, to unearth obscure historical facts, keeps me in a constant state of surprise. I commend his relentless determination to verify every detail, with local sources in Nassau's historical community, for corroboration of his findings."—Capt. Paul C. Aranha, author, THE ISLAND AIRMAN . . . AND HIS BAHAMA ISLANDS HOME.

"Eric Wiberg has made a significant contribution to the bibliography of World War II history."
—J. Revell Carr, Santa Fe, N.M.

This his book tells one more key part of the big story and is one more piece in the giant puzzle of the history of World War II. Its value for historians cannot be underestimated.

Throughout the stories of the attacks by German and Italian submarines on Allied shipping in the water around the Bahamas and the Turks and Caicos, several consistent themes emerge in Wiberg's thorough accounts. Prime among them is the heroism of the merchant mariners who time and again put themselves in danger as they performed the critical task of moving supplies, military and civilian, which were vital to ultimate victory.
We read of numerous instances of sailors having their ships shot out from under them and then continuously going back to sea and having additional ships torpedoed and sunk. We can also recognize what we know today as Post Traumatic Stress Disorder (PTSD), which was seldom recognized 75 years ago.

U-Boats in the Bahamas (HC)
by Eric Wiberg

History : Military : World War II
History : Caribbean & West Indies/General

Print price $37.95
378 Pages
ISBN: 9781899694624
Binding: B&W 6.14 x 9.21in or 234 x 156mm (Royal 8vo) Blue Cloth w/Jacket on White w/Gloss Lam

Eric Wiberg grew up in the Bahamas, the son of the Swedish Consul-General there. A licensed maritime lawyer, his thesis for a Master's Degree in Marine Affairs was published as Tanker Disasters. For three years he commercially operated tankers in Singapore. Over 25 years he has sailed on 100 vessels, most of them sailboats, for 75,000 miles, including voyages across the Atlantic and Pacific and over 30 ocean passages to or from Bermuda. He has published four books, the latest being ROUND THE WORLD IN THE WRONG SEASON. A graduate of Boston College, he studied at Harris Manchester College, Oxford, and in Lisbon. Employed in the shipping industry in New York City, he lives with his wife and son in Westport, Connecticut.

Brick Tower Press
Habent Sua Fata Libelli

Brick Tower Press
POB 342, Manhanset House
Shelter Island Hts., NY 11965-0342
bricktower@aol.com
www.BrickTowerPress.com

About the Book
Including an essay on the Constitution and Race by President Barack Obama

This edition of the United States Constitution features the complete text of the Constitution and its twenty-seven amendments in a definitive and easily read version that has been approved by leading congressional and constitutional scholars.

Illuminating this historic document are essays and commentary by some of America's leading statesmen, including President Barack Obama, Former Chief Justice Warren E. Burger, and Senator Robert Dole.

Senator Charles McC. Mathias Jr. considered by many to have been the most distinguished senatorial scholar on the Constitution, conveys the fascinating story of the Constitution in an essay that can be enjoyed by all who cherish its freedoms.

Former Speaker of the House, the late Thomas P. "Tip" O'Neill, who presided over some of the most important legislation of the twentieth century, discusses what the Constitution means to us today.

Constitution of the United States
by John Colby, David Osterlund, editors

Law : Constitutional

Print price $39.95
130 Pages
ISBN: 9781883283803

Binding: B&W 5 x 8 in or 203 x 127mm Blue Cloth w/Jacket on White w/Gloss Lam

Brick Tower Press

Habent Sua Fata Libelli

Brick Tower Press
POB 342, Manhanset House
Shelter Island Hts., NY 11965-0342
bricktower@aol.com
www.BrickTowerPress.com

About the Book

"In this practical guide, Aliette Carolan insightfully outlines the keys to a successful marriage and its dissolution. She paves the way for women, especially, to feel empowered in their life-choices which then allows them to make the best decisions for themselves and their family. This is a great guide for any woman who wants to be smart, empowered and conscious in the choices she makes in love, life and family."
—Dr. Shefali Tsabary NYT Bestselling Author of THE AWAKENED FAMILY

GIVE AWAY YOUR HEART, but don't lose your mind. Know the deal you're getting into. Know that self-preservation is the key to a happy marriage— and a happy divorce. We don't take a job expecting that we'll hate it and quit. We don't sign the lease on an apartment we'll be sick of in six months, and we don't enter into a relationship planning for the breakup. But the flip side is that we shouldn't expect any relationship we enter into will save us from the responsibility of being self-sufficient.

No matter where you are in the process—dating, engaged, married, contemplating separation, and divorce—if you can realize why you have to put yourself first, you're halfway there. Whether you're in the rapturous throes of endless love or the first moments of stomach-churning awareness that your marriage is falling apart, this book is for you. It's for every woman who understands that self-preservation will not happen if you rely on someone else to save you. You need to maintain—or begin to establish— your personal independence and financial solvency if you want to be self-sufficient no matter what life throws at you. You can lean on someone, but you have to be able to stand on your own two feet at a moment's notice, and that's what this book is about.

Just In Case! Lose Your Heart, Not Your Mind: Smart Woman's Guide to Marriage a
by Aliette Carolan

Law : Family Law - Divorce & Separation
Family & Relationships : Divorce & Separation

Print price $29.95
178 Pages
ISBN: 9781899694730
Binding: B&W 6.14 x 9.21 in or 234 x 156mm (Royal 8vo) Blue Cloth w/Jacket on White w/Gloss Lam

In a legal career spanning more than a decade, Aliette H. Carolan, Esq., an AV Rated-Preeminent Complex Marital & Family Law attorney has handled hundreds of divorce cases in Miami, Florida, a city that ranks among the top ten in the U.S. for the highest divorce rates. Ms. Carolan earned her J.D. from Nova Southeastern University in 2003 and her B.S. at the University of Miami 1999. She studied International and Comparative Law at the Paris Institute, in Paris, France, and attended the Foreign Policy Seminar at American University in Washington, D.C.

She is a member of the Florida Bar (Family Law Section); the United States District Court, Southern District of Florida; and the American Bar Association (Family Law Section and Reproductive Section) and the First Family Law Inns of Court.

Brick Tower Press
Habent Sua Fata Libelli

Brick Tower Press
POB 342, Manhanset House
Shelter Island Hts., NY 11965-0342
bricktower@aol.com
www.BrickTowerPress.com

About the Book

This is a true story of young men who fought and died for their country. It puts the reader behind the stick of a Sopwith Camel from the pilot's point of view. This is the first of two volumes.

Part One of this comprehensive study covers the life of Captain Arthur Roy Brown, who is well-known as an ace fighter pilot. The basic story is told in Brown's own words, via his previously unpublished letters home and the entries in his Pilot's Flying Log Book.

Part Two of the book covers Captain Brown's encounter with Manfred von Richthofen, the Red Baron, in detail.

In 1995 Alan Bennett toured the site in France where Captain Brown had attacked the Red Baron on 21 April, 1918. As an experienced pilot of similar aircraft, he had grave doubts as to the truth of some parts of the story. The eventual result was a book written in conjunction with Norman Franks: THE RED BARON'S LAST FLIGHT. After plentiful information from readers, Captain Roy Brown's family, and Wop May's son, plus further research in France, a considerably different picture of the entire event and of Roy Brown's life emerged. This new book, Captain Roy Brown, tells the complete definitive story.

Captain Roy Brown, a True Story of the Great War, Vol. I
by Alan D. Bennett

Library: Captain Roy Brown
Military/World War I

Print price $37.95
794 Pages
ISBN: 9781883283568
Binding: B&W 6 x 9 in or 229 x 152 mm Perfect Bound on Creme w/Matte Lam
Series Number: 1

Margaret Harmon is Captain Roy Brown's daughter. She lives in Arizona, and provided most of her father's letters. Denny May is Wilfrid "Wop" May's son. He lives in Alberta and is very active in keeping his father's legacy alive. Alan Bennett finished compiling his book on Captain Roy Brown around Christmas of 2006. He was always striving for perfection to make sure his manuscript would be as complete as possible. He received correspondence from around the world to help him in this endeavour. Though not in great health towards the end, he nevertheless continued his research with passion and zeal. Alan Bennett passed away in January 2007.

Brick Tower Press
Habent Sua Fata Libelli

Brick Tower Press
POB 342, Manhanset House
Shelter Island Hts., NY 11965-0342
bricktower@aol.com
www.BrickTowerPress.com

About the Book

This is a true story of young men who fought and died for their country. It puts the reader behind the stick of a Sopwith Camel from the pilot's point of view. This is the second of two volumes.

Part One of this comprehensive study covers the life of Captain Arthur Roy Brown, who is well-known as an ace fighter pilot. The basic story is told in Brown's own words, via his previously unpublished letters home and the entries in his Pilot's Flying Log Book.

Part Two of the book covers Captain Brown's encounter with Manfred von Richthofen, the Red Baron, in detail.

In 1995 Alan Bennett toured the site in France where Captain Brown had attacked the Red Baron on 21 April, 1918. As an experienced pilot of similar aircraft, he had grave doubts as to the truth of some parts of the story. The eventual result was a book written in conjunction with Norman Franks: THE RED BARON'S LAST FLIGHT. After plentiful information from readers, Captain Roy Brown's family, and Wop May's son, plus further research in France, a considerably different picture of the entire event and of Roy Brown's life emerged. This new book, Captain Roy Brown, tells the complete definitive story.

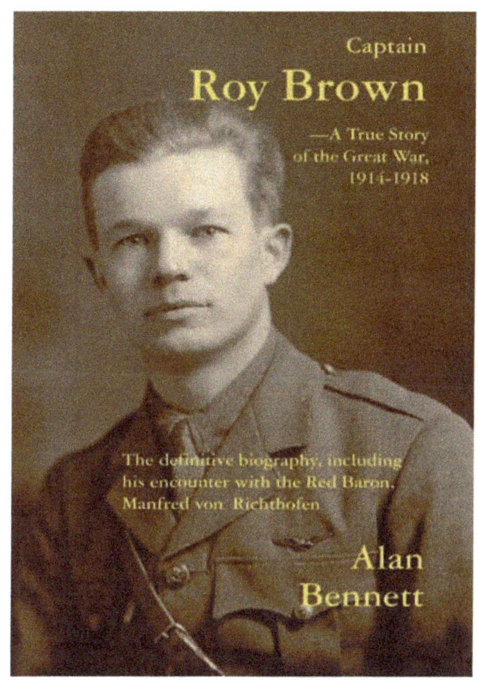

Captain Roy Brown, a True Story of the Great War, Vol. II
by Alan D. Bennett

Library: Captain Roy Brown
Military/World War I

Print price $37.95
466 Pages
ISBN: 9781883283896
Binding: B&W 6 x 9 in or 229 x 152 mm Perfect Bound on Creme w/Matte Lam
Series Number: 2

Brick Tower Press

Habent Sua Fata Libelli

Brick Tower Press
POB 342, Manhanset House
Shelter Island Hts., NY 11965-0342
bricktower@aol.com
www.BrickTowerPress.com

About the Book

"Why, in over thirty years of private practice, after listening to hundreds and hundreds of patients' dreams, had I not once encountered the presence of God, the joyful fantasy of an afterlife, the radiant appearance of an angel? Why in the outpouring and welter of wishes, secrets and hopes to which a therapist regularly attends, was heaven never mentioned?"—from the Preface

"Gerald Alper dares to enter the difficult area of spiritual, religious, nonmaterial existence. Afterlife, death and dying, relationship with God and other similar topics are presented carefully and scientifically. The book is a pleasure to read. As a former Jesuit priest (ordained in 1960), with a Magna Cum Laude and a Masters of Theology, I struggled with this issue for many years before assuming full responsibility for my beliefs. With that background I found the book refreshing, courageous, instructive and compassionate. I recommend it highly to anyone wishing to add the perspective of humanism to their religious upbringing."
—Daniel L. Araoz, Ed. D., former professor, Long Island University

"ALPER never writes dull books. He has one of the most creative analytic minds of his generation."
—Dr. Jerome David Levin, author of THE CLINTON SYNDROME

This is a book about what people in their heart of hearts, when no one is looking, believe or don't believe before organized religion, political correctness, and group pressure gathers them up in its collective grasp. It is a psychodynamic axiom that death does not exist in the unconscious. If that is true, then neither does the afterlife. Neither do angels, the pearly gates or heaven. There is, however, in addition to hope and belief, a very profound desire to be paid attention to, to be

GOD & THERAPY

What we believe when no one is watching

GERALD ALPER

GERALD ALPER is an internationally recognized psychotherapist, fellow of the American Institute for Psychotherapy & Psychoanalysis, and author of twenty books. These include, besides his celebrated PORTRAIT OF THE ARTIST AS A YOUNG PATIENT, THE PARANOIA OF EVERYDAY LIFE and THE DARK SIDE OF THE ANALYTIC MOON.

God & Therapy
by Gerald Alper

PSYCHOLOGY : Psychotherapy/General
Religion : Atheism

Print price $17.95
182 Pages
ISBN: 9781596874350
Binding: B&W 6 x 9 in or 229 x 152 mm Perfect Bound on Creme w/Gloss Lam

Brick Tower Press

Habent Sua Fata Libelli

Brick Tower Press
POB 342, Manhanset House
Shelter Island Hts., NY 11965-0342
bricktower@aol.com
www.BrickTowerPress.com

About the Book

"The deep psychodynamic digging of ALPER reaches to celebrated experiments, death in the afterlife, the mind, the interface of science and religion, and cosmos-centric issues. Readers are enriched greatly by the intellectual treasures unearthed toilsomely by the spade of psychodynamic excavator ALPER." –LEO UZYCH, JD, MPH

"ALPER never writes dull books. He has one of the most creative analytic minds of his generation."
–DR. JEROME DAVID LEVIN, author of The Clinton Syndrome

Within these pages GERALD ALPER explores the pervasive propensity among leading scientists in their quests for quantification and reductionism to overlook completely the presence of the "Elephant in the Room"–the dynamic unconscious–and the very real consequences that result when science minimizes the human equation.

Offering a holistic, contextual view of the mind and its manifestations that neither excludes nor privileges the methods of science, ALPER examines the conclusions drawn by the experimentalist by taking the laboratory and putting it back into the real world. In the process he illuminates the fallacies inherent in some of the most celebrated scientific experiments in modern times while convincingly asserting that the experiential and existential aspects of our everyday lives are no less relevant.

THE ELEPHANT IN THE ROOM

GERALD ALPER

The Elephant in the Room-The Denial of the Unconscious Mind
by Gerald Alper

PSYCHOLOGY : Psychotherapy/General

Print price $17.95
188 Pages
ISBN: 9781596879737
Binding: B&W 6 x 9 in or 229 x 152 mm Perfect Bound on White w/Gloss Lam

GERALD ALPER is an internationally recognized psychotherapist, fellow of the American Institute for Psychotherapy & Psychoanalysis, and author of twenty books. These include, besides his celebrated PORTRAIT OF THE ARTIST AS A YOUNG PATIENT, THE PARANOIA OF EVERYDAY LIFE and THE DARK SIDE OF THE ANALYTIC MOON.

Brick Tower Press
POB 342, Manhanset House
Shelter Island Hts., NY 11965-0342
bricktower@aol.com
www.BrickTowerPress.com

About the Book

James S. Cusack has been helping people addicted to alcohol and drugs for over 35 years. A recovered alcoholic himself, he started on the road to recovery in 1952 working with Alcoholics Anonymous. By embracing the self-help philosophy used in 12-Step programs, Jim has been helping people recover to this day. Detox facilities didn't exist when Jim started his work, but armed with warmth and caring, he began touching people's lives. By hard work and some rehab training courses, Jim founded Glenacre Lodge that became one of the first rehab centers of its kind. Continuing the philosophy established by his work at Glenacre Lodge, Jim founded Veritas Villa, an internationally recognized model for the treatment of alcohol and drug dependency. Among the first to become a Credentialed Alcoholism Counselor (CAC), Jim helped establish New York State requirements for alcoholism counselors.

Always Aware, A 12-Step Plan to Recovery and Healing from Alcohol & Drugs
by James S. Cusack

Self-Help : Twelve-Step Programs

Print price $15.95
200 Pages
ISBN: 9781883283070
Binding: B&W 6 x 9 in or 229 x 152 mm Perfect Bound on White w/Gloss Lam

Brick Tower Press

Habent Sua Fata Libelli

Brick Tower Press
POB 342, Manhanset House
Shelter Island Hts., NY 11965-0342
bricktower@aol.com
www.BrickTowerPress.com

About the Book

"The stricken Ferry, Samina, has disappeared beneath the waves, leaving hundreds desperate for rescue. Who would find them and how many would be saved from the storm-ridden seas? "Stone Phillips, NBC News, Dateline

"Fascinating aspects of maritime history..." Nautical Magazine

"The author has a brilliant style and explains clearly and consisely why each disaster occurred and who was to blame." This England

This book follows the changing pattern of man's fortunes at sea, from the golden age of sail, through the proud years when steam reigned supreme, to the present day, when the flag of convenience rules the waves. It tells of triumphs and disasters, some recent, some long forgotten, and illustrates how, contrary to all expectations, the fine art of seamanship has withered and died with the advent of advanced technology.

"It seemed absolute panic was about to take hold, until Major Alexander Sefton drew his sword and stepped into the pages of the history books. Calling on the troops to hold fast, Sefton, with the aid of his officers and NCOs, fell the men in on deck as though they were on a routine parade... With order restored, Captain Salmond was able to begin the evacuation of the ship. First priority was given to the women and children, who were taken off in one of the quarter boats already in the water. The second quarter boat was then brought alongside and one of the gigs successfully launched. Within a matter of minutes, the three boats were pulling away from the ship carrying eighty survivors. The boats were heavily laden, but the sea was still calm and they were in no danger." HMS Birkenhead -1852

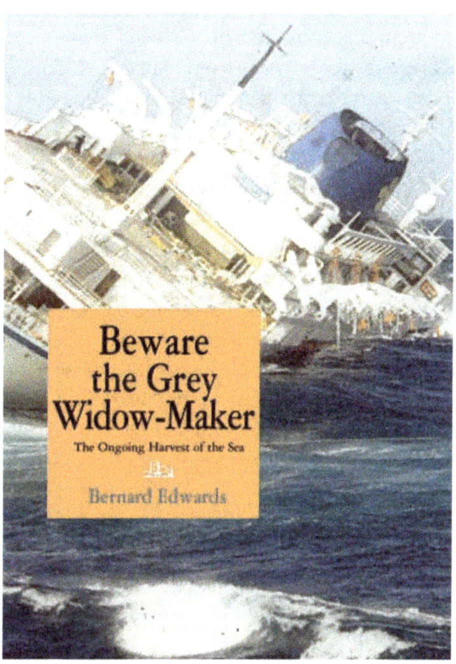

With 37 years at sea under his belt, Captain Bernard Edwards has over ten titles in print including SOS-MEN AGAINST THE SEA, BLOOD & BUSHIDO, RETURN OF THE COFFIN SHIPS, AND SALVO! A resident of Wales, Captain Edwards is close to the sea he writes about. His lifetime experience at sea enables him to add authentic touches and bring official reports to life.

Beware the Grey Widow-Maker
by Bernard Edwards

Ships & Shipbuilding/History

Print price $39.95
412 Pages
ISBN: 9781883283322

Binding: B&W 6 x 9 in or 229 x 152 mm Blue Cloth w/Jacket on White w/Gloss Lam

Brick Tower Press
Habent Sua Fata Libelli

Brick Tower Press
POB 342, Manhanset House
Shelter Island Hts., NY 11965-0342
bricktower@aol.com
www.BrickTowerPress.com

About the Book
The stories I recount in this book are true. The characters I write about are real people and in nearly every case I have used real names. Only where the event described might cause embarrassment have I used a fictitious name.

My first thought for a title was "The World Was My Ashtray," a title inspired by one of my first pursers who announced every time he opened a bottle of gin, "the world is my ash tray," at the same time throwing the cap over his shoulder, through the open porthole, into the sea. The seabed between England and Australia must be littered with his bottle tops. Readers might be given an impression that officers in passenger ships spend a great deal of time drinking. We may have entertained more than officers have time for today. I never saw anyone incapable of responding to an emergency, or a watch-keeper drinking before going on duty. I wrote this book for fun when I was missing the sea and my former shipmates. It has a taken a lot of persuasion from friends to publish this story.

ORMONDE
to
ORIANA

ORIENT LINE
to
AUSTRALIA AND BEYOND
A PURSER remembers

Nelson French

Navigator Books

Ormonde to Oriana: Orient Line to Australia and Beyond
by Nelson French

Ships & Shipbuilding/History
Biography & Autobiography : Personal Memoirs

Print price $13.95
224 Pages
ISBN: 9780902830431
Binding: B&W 6 x 9 in or 229 x 152 mm Perfect Bound on Creme w/Gloss Lam

Nelson French joined the Orient Line as an Assistant Purser when he was released from the Army in 1947. He was appointed Purser in 1954 and thereafter served in every ship of the Orient fleet. He was involved in the commissioning and the Maiden Voyage of the last great Orient Liner, ORIANA. On leaving the sea, Nelson French became a Bursar at St. Catherine's College, Oxford. He retired in 1981 and now lives in Oxfordshire.

Brick Tower Press

Habent Sua Fata Libelli

Brick Tower Press
POB 342, Manhanset House
Shelter Island Hts., NY 11965-0342
bricktower@aol.com
www.BrickTowerPress.com

About the Book

The "whole mess" as Stan put it, began on December 7, 1941, when the Japanese government attacked the United States Pacific fleet in Hawaii. On the following day the United States declared war on Japan and for those of Japanese decent, most of whom were American Citizens, life would never be the same.

Stan's diary serves as witness to a dark time in our history and is told through the eyes of a teenager who will soon be expected to take up the responsibility of a man. As you read his diary, you will discover Stan's creative talents, as well as his idealism, his optimism, and his aspirations. He has a quirky sense of humor, along with a more serious side, and dreams of a "United Nations of Earth." He talks to his diary as a confidant, a safe place to express his opinions and record the everyday events of his life. No one told him he had to keep a journal.

Stan and his family were swept up in the largest mass roundup in our country's history. On May 14, 1942 the Hayamis, along with thousands of others, were taken to the Pomona Fairgrounds, one of 16 Assembly Centers where the Nikkei (people of Japanese ancestry) were temporarily imprisoned until more permanent Relocation Centers were built. The Hayamis were moved from Pomona to Heart Mountain in Wyoming.

In November of 1942, Stan Hayami began keeping a diary that captures the harsh reality of Wyoming and his personal struggles as a student, son, brother, friend, and citizen of the world, who despite all obstacles, holds onto his dreams of the future. It is his optimism that continues to shine through his diary, and his determination to improve himself as well as the world. His dreams will continue to inspire those who work to build a world where differences are not met with racism and war, but with respect for others and kindness that allows all people to live in harmony and with dignity.

Stanley Hayami, Nisei Son: His Diary, Letters, and Story from an American Concentr
by Joanne Oppenheim, Stanley Hayami

Oppenheim is the author of more than 50 books for and about children. Her book, Dear Miss Breed (Scholastic) won the 2007 Carter G. Woodson Award of the National Council for the Social Studies. She is also the author of the Read It! Play It! series that promote literacy.

World War II, Biography
History : Military - World War II
BIOGRAPHY & AUTOBIOGRAPHY / Cultural, Ethnic & Regional / Asian & Asian Amer
Print price $19.95
204 Pages
ISBN: 9781883283674
Binding: B&W 8.25 x 11 in or 280 x 210 mm Perfect Bound on White w/Gloss Lam

Brick Tower Press

Habent Sua Fata Libelli

Brick Tower Press
POB 342, Manhanset House
Shelter Island Hts., NY 11965-0342
bricktower@aol.com
www.BrickTowerPress.com

About the Book
Where the recent movie, Chronicles of Narnia, the Lion, the Witch and the Wordrobe begins in wartime London, this book continues the real-life adventure of an actual family caught in the middle of that conflict, threading through the events of World War II. This is a plain tale of a child evacuee escaping the London blitz - and perhaps worse, if the imminence of invasion by gloating shock troops of Nazi elite is taken into account.

The author describes his journey on a Canadian-bound Atlantic convoy on a ship once commanded by his father who had been recalled to active duty. He describes the separation from his mother and life aboard ship with the German U-Boat campaign threatening the crew at every moment. The author arrives first in Boston and then travels to New Jersey to live with family friends the author's father met in New York during the First World War. The story captures the innocence of a special period in American history caught between the Great Depression and Pearl Harbor where terrible military and political events raged unabated until US entry into World War II.

In a world where national boundaries increasingly count for little more than lines on a map, its child population could also suffer evacuation to safer zones if a land war affected the country internally. For nothing now is beyond imagination in terms of terrorism in the name of culture, not a country. As a child evacuee to America in a global political climate not unlike the present, the author chose an option–he would avoid the horrors which ultimately proved the lot of Europe's children had Britain not missed being overrun by a whisker.

Visiting New York three weeks after "nine-eleven"; aware of the city's spontaneous official and citizen response among numbing scenes, was to return

The American Option

Philip Morgan Cheek

The American Option, And, Yes, I Almost Became an American
by Philip Cheek

World War II, Biography

Print price $18.95
238 Pages
ISBN: 9781883283407
Binding: B&W 6 x 9 in or 229 x 152 mm Perfect Bound on White w/Matte Lam

www.ingramcontent.com/pod-product-compliance
Lightning Source LLC
LaVergne TN
LVHW080328110826
845155LV00026B/222